S. Law

Áral Sea

W9-DGF-822

Caspian Sea

ck   Sea

•Boğazköy

URARTU

Lake Van

Lake Urmia

•Kültepe

HITTITES

•Karatepe

Carchemish

Tigris

•Nineveh

ASSYRIANS

Shargat (Ashur)

•Behistun

CYPRUS

Ugarit

alion

Arwad

•Hamath

AKKADIANS

Kition

Euphrates

•Baghdad

Byblos

Sidon

Babylon

Tyre

PHOENICIANS

BABYLONIANS

Nippur

Lagash

Uruk

SUMER

Pasargade

etta   PALESTINE

Dead Sea

Ur

Naqsh-e-Rustam

CANAAN

SUMERIANS

Persepolis

ta

SINAI

Persian Gulf

Tel el-Amarna

EGYPT

Red Sea

•Karnak

•Philae Is.

Abu Simbel

FORGOTTEN SCRIPTS

FORGOTTEN SCRIPTS

How they were deciphered and their
impact on contemporary culture

CYRUS H. GORDON

BASIC BOOKS, INC., PUBLISHERS
New York

417
G

TO MY WIFE
JOAN
who understands
the long frustrations
and sudden joys
of cryptanalysis

PREFACE

The nineteenth and twentieth centuries have been an age of scientific progress beyond the dreams of man in earlier periods. Sumero-Akkadian mythology tells us of a hero, Etana, who flew heavenward on the back of an eagle, and Greek mythology relates how Daedalus made wings so that he and his son Icarus could fly through the air; but what pre-modern man ever conceived of the spacecraft now circling the earth or reaching the moon, with ever-greater achievements unfolding in rapid succession? Nor are the miracles in other branches of modern science less remarkable. What is less well known is that there are comparably great achievements in the humanities that started in the nineteenth century and are continuing with unabated progress today.

With the passing of antiquity in Roman times, Western civilization came to be conceived as starting with the three classical forms of Mediterranean culture—Israel, Greece, and Rome. Homer and the Bible stood at the beginning of recorded history, and everything earlier was regarded as prehistoric. And yet a succession of travelers and curious intellectuals knew that in Egypt and Iran there were monuments and inscriptions of a distant past. Less spectacular to the visitor's eye were the ruined cities of Mesopotamia, but they were none the less associated with cuneiform texts that concealed an ancient story. Hebrew, Greek, and Latin literature preserved enough collateral information to provide the future decipherers with the necessary background. All that was needed was the men with the dream, the dedication, the knowledge, the mind, and the courage to persevere in the search for truth.

We are about to tell the story of how forgotten scripts were deciphered and lost languages recovered, adding two thousand years to the documented span of Western civilization. Greece and Israel no longer stand at the dawn of history. Thanks to the decipherment of Egyptian and cuneiform, there are now fifteen centuries of recorded history in the cradle of Western culture, before the Greeks and the Hebrews appear on the scene. Moreover, the earliest inscriptions pertaining to the Hellenes and Israelites antedate the composition of the *Iliad* and of Genesis.

The desire to solve the mystery of esoteric inscriptions is almost as old as writing itself. The most familiar legend of decipherment appears in the Book of Daniel: Once upon a time Belshazzar of Babylon was confronted with a mysterious message wondrously inscribed by a disembodied hand upon his palace wall. None of the sages could decipher it except Daniel, who by divine inspiration read the Aramaic text *mene mene tekel upharsin* and without hesitation interpreted it flawlessly.[1] The modern decipherer, like Daniel, needs inspiration, but unlike Daniel he also requires a background in philology and history. Technologically the decipherers of cuneiform and hieroglyphic texts resemble Daniel somewhat as the Wright brothers resemble Etana and Daedalus.

The decipherments of the forgotten scripts in the cradles of Western culture have not only revealed millennia of history; they have also opened a Pandora's Box of problems that may prove to be more difficult to solve than the decipherments. While Darwinism was hitting at what eighteenth-century rationalism had left of traditional religion, the cuneiform texts revealed a pagan mythology that was used as ammunition to blow up the vestiges of biblical faith. If Noah's flood was only a late Hebrew copy of the ancient Babylonian deluge, what could one still accept in Sacred Scripture? The net result was a tendency to split the public into two opposing camps: atheists and obscurantists. The one maintained that science and archeological discovery exposed religious tradition as fallacy and fraud. The other rejected the testimony of science and the newly deciphered texts as pernicious. We are still suffering from this needless dichotomy, which has bred a lost generation seeking meaning in history and life.

The illogical crisis came in the Scopes trial, with two remarkable men—the atheist Clarence Darrow and the "defender of the faith" William Jennings Bryan—championing the op-

---

[1] Daniel 5, where the interest in the text is to interpret a prophecy that would otherwise remain secret. Today our interest in inscriptions is rather for the information they provide on the past. Somewhat similarly, the ancients interpreted dreams as announcements of, or advice on, things to come, whereas we interpret dreams as reflexes of past experience.

posing viewpoints. It was not necessary then, as it is not necessary now, to reject either scientific enlightenment or our traditional heritage. To be civilized and complete, we must accept scientific enlightenment and our traditional heritage, each in its proper place. Neglect of either is disastrous. Science without tradition can produce technicians but not cultured men; tradition without science can breed learned but not rational men.

The succession of decipherers whose work has revolutionized the humanities was the product of an intellectual atmosphere that we may trace to the Renaissance. That rebirth embodied an interest in the ancient past. Although it stressed the classical heritage of Greece and Rome, the preoccupation of artists and scholars with Scripture kept the Bible lands in the picture. Moreover, there was a growing curiosity about the world as a whole, culminating in the Age of Discovery. The voyages of Columbus and Magellan and other pioneers in sailing the seven seas and exploring distant shores were not merely the result of improved technical capabilities; they were also the product of the enlarged frame of mind in Western Europe, ushered in by the Renaissance.

The immediate prologue of the Age of the Decipherments is the Enlightenment of the eighteenth century. The excavation of Herculaneum and Pompeii then raised the interest in archeology and ancient texts to new heights.[2] Intellectual curiosity had added oriental studies to the university repertoire. Travelers like Carsten Niebuhr (1733–1815) visited the cradles of Western civilization and brought back and published fac-

[2] For readable introductions to the subject, see Leo Deuel, *Testaments of Time* (New York: Alfred A. Knopf, 1965), pp. 55–77; and C. W. Ceram, *Hands on the Past* (New York: Alfred A. Knopf, 1966), pp. 61–68 (selected from the writings of J. J. Winkelmann and A. Goldsmidt).

similes of inscriptions in forgotten scripts. The interest in far-
away places peers through the literature of the times. Samuel
Johnson's *Rasselas* is set in Abyssinia. Voltaire's satirical stories
unfold in distant lands, ranging from Babylon to the New
World. A constellation of interests and activities was pointing toward the decipherments of the nineteenth century.
Archeology, in the form of both exploration and excavation,
was under way. Texts as well as monuments were reaching
Europe from the lands of the forgotten scripts. The study of
Arabic, Syriac, Coptic, Ethiopic, and other Near Eastern
languages was being increasingly added to the old repertoire
of Hebrew, Greek, and Latin. European involvement in India
had led to the study of Sanskrit and the ancient Persian texts
of the Parsees.

At the close of the eighteenth century, Napoleon, with an
eye on far-off India, embarked on the invasion of Egypt to
open a new era. He catapulted the Near East into its modern
period, which is characterized by Western European influence. He also initiated the age of large-scale collecting, studying, and publishing of nonclassical inscriptions, art, and
architecture. Specifically, he ushered in the age of Egyptology.

While Napoleon's invasion of Egypt was more spectacular
than events in western Iran, where the Achaemenian kings had
left their inscriptions, the cuneiform materials had been discovered and some of the men destined to decipher them had
been born during the last third of the eighteenth century.

The open-mindedness and intellectual curiosity of that age
were, as always, too much for reactionary men. Both fundamentalisms—secular and religious—gained in momentum when
confronted with new developments. Secular fundamentalism
stemmed (and still stems) largely from classicists who object
to giving credit to the "barbaric" civilizations such as the

Egyptians or Phoenicians. Religious fundamentalism is opposed to connections between the Chosen People and their
heathen neighbors. Both fundamentalisms are essentially the
same, prompted as they are by the desire to keep an ideal free
of outside contamination. Classical fundamentalism was un-
leashed after Champollion's decipherment of Egyptian. Religious fundamentalism broke loose with renewed vigor after
the announcement of the biblical parallels in cuneiform literature.

The intellectual life of the West took a strange turn by the
end of the nineteenth century. Hitherto, fully educated men
had tried to reckon with Hebrew, Greek, and Latin as their
threefold heritage. In the poems of Milton we see the blending
at every turn. For a long time after Harvard University was
founded in the seventeenth century, the valedictorian address
was delivered in Hebrew. The Yale emblem still carries its
Hebrew as well as Latin text. But with the growth of knowledge in the nineteenth century, specialization had begun to
separate classics from Hebrew. The intellectuals reared in
the classical tradition were committed to the uniqueness of
the Greek and Roman ideal, but at the same time, as long
as they professed to be Christians, they were forced to reckon
with the divine inspiration of the Bible. How were they to
cling to a twofold ideal, which they themselves held to be in
opposition? Artificial barriers were accordingly erected as
people reasoned somewhat as follows: "The Hebrew was a
genius in religion and morality even as the Greek was a genius
in philosophy and science. The one was spiritual and oriental;
the other was rational and European."

The net result was that instead of being Mediterranean
peoples flourishing during the same centuries, Greeks and
Hebrews were so separated by a contrived chasm that they

might just as well have been from opposite poles if not from different planets. This led to a kind of truce: Since two different groups of scholars foster classics and Old Testament studies, respectively, each is to help preserve the peace by staying in his own terrain. The classicist does not as a rule welcome any evidence of profound Phoenician impact on Greece, and the well-adjusted Hebrew scholar is quite content to shut his eyes to Mycenaean and Minoan developments even though he knows that Palestine is named after an Aegean people called the Philistines.

Thus, the Enlightenment of the eighteenth century has left us a twofold legacy—the expanding mentality which produced the decipherments and the reaction which not only prescribes blinkers but resists the mounting evidence of mutual relationships and a common heritage in the ancient Mediterranean.

March 1968   CYRUS H. GORDON

CONTENTS

ILLUSTRATIONS

(following page 86)

FORGOTTEN SCRIPTS

1

CODES
AND
CIPHERS

There is a professional world of codes and ciphers that has evolved an elaborate science and technology of its own. Every government and many private agencies use secret writing for their classified communications. There are differences between solving forgotten scripts and modern cryptography. Forgotten scripts were not written to defy interpretation to all but the writer and the receiver; they were meant to be intelligible to the entire literate public.

However, the methods employed in solving enemy systems of cryptography are of great value to the decipherer of ancient scripts, and it is not surprising that since World War I some of the successful decipherments have been made by scholars who have had experience in military cryptanalysis. Accordingly, a survey of the elements of cryptography will help us understand the decipherment of the ancient systems.

Codes and ciphers are two different forms of cryptography. Codes deal with the substitution of whole words or even phrases. By merely taking a dictionary and writing in a code number next to each word, we can transform the dictionary into a code book. For example if the dictionary lists more than 9,999 words but not more than 99,999, a five-digit code is indicated. If the dictionary starts: *a, aback, abacus, abandon, abandoned, abase, abashed, abate, abbess, abbey, abbot, abbreviate, abbreviation, abdicate,* . . . , we can assign the following code numbers:

a	00001	abbess	00009
aback	00002	abbey	00010
abacus	00003	abbot	00011
abandon	00004	abbreviate	00012
abandoned	00005	abbreviation	00013
abase	00006	abdicate	00014
abashed	00007	. . .	. . .
abate	00008		

The same book can be used for encoding and decoding messages because the sequence of the numbers follows the alphabetized words. This is therefore called a one-part code. Inherently, it is not good for secrecy, because as soon as the codebreakers realize its nature, they can interpolate values. Thus, when they discover that 00001 is "*a*," they immediately have reason to believe that they are faced with a one-part code. If they solve any two code numbers (e.g., 00005 = "abandon" and 00014 = "abdicate"), they know that an intermediate number comes between the two in the dictionary (e.g., 00008 comes after "abandon" but before "abdicate").

A two-part code requires two different books: one in dictionary order for encoding and one with the code numbers in numerical order for decoding. Our encoding book could begin thus:

a	66789
aback	12834
abacus	92386
abandon	04200

Here there is no relation between the order of the code numbers and the alphabetized dictionary. The decoding book might begin thus:

00001	country
00002	fifteen
00003	debate
00004	zebra
00005	abandon
00006	escalate
. . .	. . .

The two-part code is a more secure system, but the preparation and distribution of the extra code books cost time and money. It pays to employ them only if they are used for reasonably long periods. Any code that is used extensively is vulnerable, however, because it is a law of secret writing that if the enemy intercepts enough of it, he can solve the system and reconstruct the code book through statistics and analysis.

For in any language, the frequency and position of certain words provide the code breaker with ways of transforming coded messages into plain text.

Something else that makes codes vulnerable is spies and agents who steal, buy, or photocopy code books.

We might also note that codes (particularly commercial codes) are sometimes designed not for secrecy but to save on cablegram expenses. If "05638" means "Sell immediately the stock mentioned in your letter which we have just received," the cable or telegram will cost less than the full plain-text message. When we write the French abbreviation "R.S.V.P." after an invitation, we are doing something similar; it is a short way of saying, "Please tell us whether you will attend."

For maintaining secrecy, ciphers are generally used. Either the plain text or a coded message can be enciphered. Let us say that the following message is encoded in accordance with a two-part system thus:[1]

Plain text:	ENEMY PLANS ATTACK AT-DAWN		
Encoded text:	0931	5723 6288	9482

There is no reason to be sure that the enemy does not possess our code books, which have been in use for a long time. Accordingly, our cryptographic security staff has decided to protect our communications by agreeing (let us say) to add 15 to the first group, 162 to the second, 1903 to the third, and then begin all over again (adding first 15, then 162, and finally 1903, etc.).

Coded message:	0931	5723	6288	9482
Encipherment:	+15	+162	+1903	+15
Cryptogram:	0946	5885	8191	9497

[1] Since a code book for simple messages in the field need not have more than 9,999 words or phrases, four-digit groups will suffice.

The receiver gives the cryptogram to his cryptographer, who first deciphers it (i.e., by subtracting the encipherment) and then decodes the deciphered message into plain text.

The above type of encipherment is called an "additive." It can, of course, be applied directly to the plain text. Suppose our encipherment is "1-2-3"; i.e., we shall add 1 to the first letter, 2 to the second letter, and 3 to the third letter, and then begin over again (adding 1 to the fourth letter, 2 to the fifth letter, and 3 to the sixth, etc.).

Plain text:	ENEMY PLANS ATTACK A T DAWN
Encipherment:	1 2 3 1 2 3 1 2 3 1 2 3 1 2 3 1 2 3 1 2 3 1
Cryptogram:	FPHNA SMCQT CWUCFL CW ECZO

When we add 1 to *e*, we go to the next letter in the alphabet (*f*); when we add 2 to *n*, we go on to the second letter thereafter (*p*); 3 added to *e* means the third letter thereafter (*h*).

Another kind of encipherment is transposition. For instance, we can interchange the positions of the letters in every pair of letters:

Plain text:	ENEMYPLANSATTACKATDAWN
Cryptogram:	NEMEPYALSNTAATKCTAADNW

Here the cryptographer who deciphers the message will have to divide the plain text into words after transposing the cryptogram into plain text.

The simplest kind of encipherment is monoalphabetic substitution. This means that each letter is always replaced by another definite letter:

Plain alphabet:	ABCDEF GHIJKLM NOPQR STUV WXYZ
Cipher alphabet:	ZXCVBNMASDFG H JKLPO IUYT REWQ

Taking the same plain text, we have

ENEMY PLANS ATTACK AT DAWN

the cryptogram is now

BJBHW LGZJI ZUUZCF ZU VZRJ

The cryptographer charged with deciphering this message will use the following chart (in which the cipher is alphabetized while the plain values now seem randomized):

Cipher alphabet: ABCDEFGH I J KLMNOPQR STUVWXYZ

Plain alphabet: HECJXKLMSN OPG FRQZWIVTDY BUA

Monoalphabetic substitution is easy to solve because in any known language the letters have known frequencies. A couple of pages enciphered by this method can be solved without any difficulty provided the language is known. Shorter cryptograms are harder to solve because, without volume, statistics are not reliable. We shall take an example of monoalphabetic substitution in order to illustrate what methods can be used in addition to statistics. The following cryptogram is to be deciphered into plain English:

VHBSJU XBT BDDJEFOUBMMZ EJTDPWFSFE CZ
B QFBTBOU JO OJOFUFFO IVOESFE BOE
UXFOUZFJHIU IF QMPXFE JOUP B NZDFOBFB
UPNC BOE VOXJUUJOHMZ PQFOFE VQ B
OFX FSB PG EJTDPWFSZ

A frequency count tells us each letter is used so many times:

A	B	C	D	E	F	G	H	I	J	K	L	M
0	14	2	5	10	19	1	3	3	10	0	0	4

N	O	P	Q	R	S	T	U	V	W	X	Y	Z
2	17	7	4	0	5	4	11	4	2	5	0	6

It will be noted that some letters are of high frequency, others are of low frequency; the rest are in between. If we had a long cryptogram, we could solve the problem statistically without more ado. But in so short a text, statistics are not reliable. We note, however, that the letters of highest frequency are F and O (F, 19 times; and O, 17). One of these should be the letter *e*, which occurs more often than any other letter in English. We may expect the definite article "the" to occur in any English utterance, even if it be limited to a few lines. The three-letter words in the cryptogram are XBT, BOE (which occurs twice), OFX, and FSB. Disappointingly, none of these ends in F or O, and we conclude that, against all expectation, "the" does not appear in our message.

There is a one-letter word (B) that occurs three times, and it is a letter of great frequency. Now there are only two common words that we need consider (for "O" is hardly used nowadays): "a" and "I." This letter happens to begin the three-letter word BOE, which occurs twice. There are many three-letter words beginning with *a* in English, but none is more common than "and." If BOE = "and," we have B = *a*, O = *n* and E = *d*. We shall apply these values and see if they yield good or bad readings elsewhere in the cryptogram. It will be noted that four words end in FE:

EJTDPWFSFE

IVOESFE

QMPXFE

PQFOFE

Since F is of the highest frequency (occurring 19 times) and we ruled out O = *e*, F should be *e*, giving us the suffix FE =-*ed* to indicate the past tense of verbs. Since the two-letter word JO ends with *n*, the first letter must be a vowel, and *a* is ruled out because B = *a*. This leaves *i* and *o* as the only possibilities, since "an," "in," and "on" are the only two-letter English words ending in *n*. Now, in OJOFUFFO, J = *o* would yield *noneUeen*, which is meaningless in English whatever value we ascribe to U; however, $J = i$ allows us to take *nineUeen* as the only possible word in English—"nineteen"—showing that $U = t$. From this point on, the rest is easy. JOUP $= int-$ can only be "into" with $P = o$. PQFOFE $= oQened$ must be "opened" with $Q = p$. VQ $= Vp$ can only be "up" with $V = u$. QFBTBOU $= peaTant$ must be "peasant" with $T = s$. The skeleton of the number "nineteen IuOdSed and tXentZeiHIt" would not puzzle any cryptanalyst very long. It can only be "nineteen hundred and twenty-eight," which yields $I = h$, $O = n$, $S = r$, $X = w$, $Z = y$, $H = g$. With these values, we can decipher our cryptogram to this extent:

```
VHBSJU XBT BDDJEFOUBMMZ EJTDPWFSFE CZ B
u  arit was a     identa    y dis  o  ered  y a
QFBTBOU JO OJOFUFFO IVOESFE BOE
peas an t  in  nin et een  hundred  an d
UXFOUZFJHIU IF QMPXFE JOUP B NZDFOBFBO
t wen ty eigh t  he  p  owed  into a   y  enaean
UPNC BOE VOXJUUJOHMZ PQFOFE VQ B OFX
t o    and unwit t in    y opened up  a  new
FSB PG EJTDPWFSZ
era o   dis  o   ery
```

From this point the reader should be able to solve the rest. The plain text is given at the end of the chapter so that he may check his solution.

The world of cryptography is now quite complex. Encipherments that go in a cycle of three are easy to break because sooner or later the same words will reappear at the same point in the cycle, and once the cyclicity is solved, all the cryptanalyst needs is enough volume of intercepts to crack the system. Even a cycle of 100 is not enough to protect a system that is used extensively. Security may now be sought by cycles that do not repeat until the million mark is passed. This can be done through complex machines; the sender and receiver have the same adjustable machines. The receiver must also know how to set his cryptographic machine to remove the encipherment. Such systems are difficult, if not impossible, to break by cryptanalysis. Espionage or some other kind of skulduggery can be more effective. Fortunately for our purposes, we do not have to delve into the highly complex mechanical and electronic methods of encipherment and decipherment. The ancient scripts that had to be deciphered were not secret systems devised to defy reading. They were made to be read and understood. The methods used to decode and decipher help us unravel the reading and translation of forgotten scripts and languages, but nothing that has come down to us from antiquity was enciphered by an electronic randomizer so that we require a complex device for unscrambling ancient·cryptograms.

We must now differentiate the cryptographer from the cryptanalyst. The cryptographer uses the code books and cipher systems of his office. He does not handle enemy messages that require solution without benefit of code books and cipher keys. The cryptanalyst, on the other hand, deals precisely with messages that he must solve through analysis without code books and cipher keys. It is his business to decipher enemy cryptograms even if he has to break systems and reconstruct code books in the process. Our subject deals with decipherers whose role is like the cryptanalyst's rather than the cryptographer's.

Sometimes ancient texts are equipped with word dividers, which makes the task easier. But if the word dividers are not supplied, the decipherer has to edit his text and, by studying the repetitions, can break up the text into its component words. For instance, if the preceding sentence were run together, a study of it would reveal that the sequence *the* occurs no less than four times and should therefore be some common word. If there is enough text, the words can be isolated even though they be run together. In Akkadian—one of the best known of the deciphered languages—words are not separated.

Collateral information is of prime importance in starting a decipherment as well as in interpreting a text even after the opening wedge has been made. If an enciphered message from Teheran is intercepted on a certain date, it may be assumed that it is written in Persian and deals with something that belongs to our world as revealed in *The New York Times* or the Teheran newspapers of that date. If a long cryptogram is sent from Paris to every French embassy at about the time De Gaulle takes some major step or makes some notable pronouncement, two assumptions can be made: (1) that the cryptogram is in French and (2) that it deals with the news item from Paris that has just made the headlines. It has happened that codes and ciphers have been compromised by careless cryptographic clerks who have encoded and enciphered long dispatches whose plain texts have been published in the press. One of the rules of security in such cases is always to paraphrase and transpose the original before sending it as a cryptogram. Careless clerks are God's gift to the cryptanalyst charged with breaking foreign systems.[2]

The problem that confronts the decipherer of ancient texts is that even if he correctly guesses what language they are in, he has no *New York Times* to tell him what the writers may have had on their minds when they composed the inscriptions. The collateral information may, however, be supplied from

[2] One of the commonest *faux pas* made by cryptographic clerks is to insert proper names in plain text. This gives the enemy the opening wedge for deciphering the cryptogram by providing him with a clue to the context. It is interesting to note that proper names are the most frequent keys to the decipherment of ancient scripts.

history. Herodotus' genealogical facts concerning the Achaemenian kings supplied the decipherers with the data they needed for cracking the cuneiform inscriptions of Persia and Mesopotamia. A knowledge of place names is also important. That "Knossos" should be found in the Linear B texts from Knossos but not from Pylos and that "Pylos" should be found in the Linear B texts from Pylos but not from Knossos were correct assumptions that helped crack Linear B.

Not only are the names of kings and places important, but any knowledge one has of what was in the ancient scribe's mind and how he would be likely to express it can also help in deciphering ancient texts. There is a huge mass of ancient Near Eastern inscriptions that provide us with collateral information. By drawing on his knowledge of the language and of the collateral information, the decipherer can make inferences which may turn out to be right because they fit into some pattern inherent in the text. In a group of words that looked like cardinal numerals, the decipherers of Ugaritic rightly decided that the one with the pattern XYX had to be _tlt_, "three." None of the other cardinal numbers in Northwest Semitic fits this pattern.

Guesses of this kind are necessary, but they cannot be off the top of one's head; to be successful, they must reckon with the realities, or at least the probabilities, of the text to be deciphered. Even then most guesses are wrong, so that a prime quality in the cryptanalyst or decipherer is flexibility. Wrong guesses are usually exposed as incorrect by the fact that they lead to impossible combinations when applied elsewhere in the texts to be deciphered. But it is also necessary to follow through with the truth if a successful decipherment is to be achieved. Both Evans and Cowley individually got correct Greek values for Mycenaean words but they were not in a frame of mind to follow through. Evans had committed himself to a false premise (that the language was not Greek) and could not extricate himself. Without flexibility, decipherment is impossible. Guesses must be made, and it is the lucky guess that pays off. But for every lucky guess, hundreds of wrong ones must be scrapped.

Lucky guesses often take the form of the "probable word." Some three-letter combination in texts from Canaan ought to be b^el "Baal" (the well-known Canaanite god). Bauer, having determined the b and the l spotted bXl as "Baal" and obtained the correct ^{e} value for X. His guess of the probable word turned out to be right, for $X = {^e}$ makes sense in all the other combinations.

We now must define what we mean by a "decipherment." Strictly speaking, the term applies to obtaining from scratch the pronunciation of the symbols in texts that cannot even be pronounced before the decipherment. Examples of this are afforded by the decipherment of Egyptian hieroglyphs, Old Persian cuneiform, the Cypriote syllabary, and the Ugaritic cuneiform alphabet. "Decipherment" does not imply that the language turns out to be new. The Cypriote texts turned out to be Greek; the Ugaritic language is close to Hebrew. The decipherment in both cases was successful because the language was known. The basic achievement of the decipherers was to determine the pronunciation of the symbols.

A different sort of accomplishment is the working out of a new language written in a known script. Sumerian did not have to be deciphered in the sense that Akkadian did; Sumerian is written in the same script, and Akkadian was worked out first. Since Akkadian belongs to the well-established Semitic family of languages, it has been recovered with a high degree of finesse, so that scholars are in agreement as to how any but the most problematic texts are to be translated. This is still not so with Sumerian, where the handful of top authorities do not always agree in translating many passages in the most familiar literary texts (such as Gudea's Cylinders) that have been known for over half a century and republished many times.

In most essentials, of course, there is agreement in translating Sumerian texts, and the language whose very existence was unsuspected when Rawlinson began his work is now richly documented. Sumerology fills libraries with tomes of autographed texts, translations, linguistic studies, and historical works. It has therefore been "deciphered," but no one person can be credited with its decipherment. The phonetic values of Sumerian signs came out of the decipherment and study of Akkadian; countless lexical and other school texts (including bilinguals) prepared in antiquity provide the firm basis for working out the vocabulary and grammar of Sumerian. And even so, with such an abundance of materials, it is taking a long time to refine Sumerology to a point where it can be reduced to clear rules with the modicum of agreement among the experts necessary to dispel confusion from the beginning student's mind.

In the case of Hittite, we have a duplex problem because it is written in two different scripts: cuneiform and pictograms. It was Bedřich Hrozný who established the Indo-European character of Hittite, thus setting Hittitology on its right course. The cuneiform script is Sumero-Akkadian and Hrozný did not have to figure out what the signs meant phonetically. The decipherment of Cuneiform Hittite resembles not the decipherment of Old Persian but rather the "decipherment" of Sumerian. The decipherment of pictographic Hittite (officially called Hieroglyphic Hittite) is, however, a true decipherment, for the phonetic values of the signs had to be worked out from scratch. There are such dialectal differences between Cuneiform and Hieroglyphic Hittite that our detailed knowledge of Cuneiform Hittite does not always clarify linguistic problems in the hieroglyphic variety.

To understand the fundamental difference between script and language, it may be of use to make a few observations on some modern forms of writing and speech. Finnish and Chinese are two languages equally unintelligible to the average English-speaking person. Finnish is written in familiar Latin characters, so that we have no problem in knowing the sound conveyed by each letter. With Chinese, however, the pronunciation of the signs is as obscure as the meaning of the words and sentences, even if we could pronounce the text. Suppose we had to decipher both Finnish and Chinese. The magnitude of the two tasks would be different. With Chinese, script and language would have to be solved, with Finnish, only the language. Both tasks are of types that are generally called "decipherment," but they are, as we have seen, of different orders.

There is still another kind of "decipherment": when the script is known but not the identity of the language, which, however, may turn out to be a known language once it is identified. For example, texts in Greek letters were found at El-Hofra in Algeria.[3] Since the language was not Greek and the town was Punic, it was immediately surmised that the texts were Punic. Their contents are so familiar from Punic inscriptions that no alternative view had to be considered. But it took three-quarters of a century to identify the Phoenician inscriptions in Greek letters from Crete. Shall we call such a feat a "decipherment" when in retrospect it seems so simple? To achieve it, it was, in fact, necessary to "decipher"

[3] For selected texts and bibliography, see C. H. Gordon, *Supplements to Vetus Testamentum* (Leiden: Brill, 1963), IX, 22–23.

the parent language on Crete, namely, Minoan. But is the identification and description of the Minoan language a "decipherment"? After all, the script is essentially the same as the Greek Linear B. But then again, should we even call the solution Linear B a "decipherment"? For it turns out that the language and the system of writing are essentially the same as the Cypriote Greek texts written syllabically and deciphered by George Smith in 1872. By asking these questions we have answered them. The nuances and technical distinctions are endless, and we serve no useful purpose by hyperfinesse in our terminology. No two decipherments are exactly the same. We need only recognize that either scripts or languages or both can be known, partly known, or unknown. Moreover, even the identification of the language can be important because it can make the difference between intelligibility and mystery. When any person takes the first and critical steps to transform a category of "mysterious" inscriptions into intelligible documents by revealing their script or language, we shall call the achievement a "decipherment."

Every problem in this book has been simplified. If we should follow step by step how each solution was achieved, it would be like recording every motion a baby made from birth until its first successful attempt at walking. We are concerned here primarily with success rather than with preparation or with failure.

It is exceedingly hard to establish priorities in every case. Usually somebody else anticipated So-and-so in some way or other. Books are written about whether Columbus was really the discoverer of America. This book is not about whether Champollion really was the decipherer of Egyptian. We shall not wittingly cheat anyone of his due, but neither shall we be preoccupied with every "if" and "but" in our account. Decipherers, like all discoverers, want the credit for having gotten there first. Dated publications settle priority in one sense (and an important one at that), but what are we to think when A has published what he had already heard from B or found out concerning B's work? We shall touch on such problems, for they are of historic interest, but we leave their detailed analysis to others.

SOLUTION OF CRYPTOGRAM ON PAGE 8

The plain text is: "Ugarit was accidentally discovered by a peasant in nineteen hundred and twenty-eight. He plowed into a Mycenaean tomb and unwittingly opened up a new era of discovery."

Each letter was represented by the next one in the alphabet:

Cipher alphabet: ABCDEFGHIJKLMNOPQRSTUVWXYZ
Plain alphabet: z a b c d e f g h i j k l m n o p q r s t u v w x y

An experienced cryptanalyst, after determining the first few values, would detect the system (i.e., each letter is substituted by the following letter in the alphabet). Determining the system usually precedes any successful decipherment.

2

THE
DECIPHERMENT
OF EGYPTIAN

Sometime around 3000 B.C. writing was invented and developed in the Near East. There is reason to believe that it first became established in Mesopotamia, but the idea soon spread to Egypt.[1] The cuneiform of Mesopotamia has little obvious resemblance to the hieroglyphs of Egypt, and yet their principles are so similar that

[1] Henri Frankfort, *The Birth of Civilization in the Near East* (New York: Doubleday Anchor, 1956), pp. 121–37.

there must be a connection, through stimulus diffusion; i.e., the Egyptians did not copy the actual signs of Mesopotamian writing but only applied the same basic ideas. First, they established a large, but none the less limited, repertoire of pictographic signs. For example, they not only had a general sign for MAN but a number of other pictographs of men doing various things or in various states. Thus, there might be a man eating, but there would not be different signs for a man eating each kind of food or different signs for a man engaged in various aspects of eating such as biting, chewing, or swallowing. If we draw each specific object or act, we are not writing but engaging in representational art. To be useful, any system of writing must limit its number of symbols.

The next principle (in both cuneiform and hieroglyphs) is that the pictograph can stand for the sound of what is drawn, without reference to its meaning. To take some simulated English examples by way of illustration: the MAN pictograph could stand not only for "a man" but for the syllable *man;* even as the picture of a DATE could refer not only to "a date" but to the syllable *date.* Thus, the two pictographs MAN–DATE could be pronounced *man-date* and mean "a mandate." This is the most important and basic aspect of cuneiform and hieroglyphic writing; they are essentially phonetic systems even though as a rule the signs stood originally for words or ideas. As we follow the history of writing, we shall observe that the trend has been to abandon word-signs and concentrate on sound-signs.

The third principle common to Mesopotamia and Egypt is the use of determinatives, or signs that tell the category of the word. For example, there is no way of telling whether the isolated word spelled *sš* in Egyptian means "a scribe" or "a document." Accordingly, the Egyptians added the pictogram

MAN when it means "scribe" but the pictogram SCROLL when it means "document." Thus, [glyphs] *sš*, "document," but [glyphs] *sš*, "scribe."

Both cuneiform and hieroglyphs use phonetic complements to fix the sound of a sign. To take an Egyptian example: a certain bird pictogram, usually identified as GUINEA FOWL, has the reading *nḥ*. It can serve as the ideogram for the bird in question, but it can also be used as a phonogram, in which case it may be both preceded and followed by phonetic complements: *ⁿ*GUINEA FOWL*ḥ*, which can be used to express words that have nothing whatever to do with a bird and which we may represent thus: *ⁿnḥʰ*. Now there is a verb *nḥ(i)*, "to pray," whose meaning puts it in a category of words that the Egyptians indicate by the determinative of a man pointing to his mouth. The verb "to pray" can be written *ⁿnḥʰ* followed by that determinative. [glyphs] . This kind of writing often makes Egyptian easy to read and translate, for the word is written alphabetically ([glyphs] *n-ḥ*) and syllabically ([glyphs] *nḥ*), and its semantic category is indicated by the determinative [glyph] .

It remains to add that numerals are often written ideographically down to our own times: I = "one"; II = "two"; III = "three" are similar in appearance in cuneiform (**𐤔𐤔𐤔**) , hieroglyphs (III), and Latin. All our numerical symbols, indeed, are ideographic. Thus, 4 stands for the idea of fourness; its pronunciation depends entirely on the language of the text in which it appears ("four" in English but "quatre" in French).

From about 3000 B.C. until the end of the fourth century

A.D., Egyptian was written in hieroglyphs in an unbroken tradition. The large number of signs and the numerous conventional spellings required long training for the chosen few who achieved literacy.[2] In the wake of Alexander's conquest, the Greek alphabet spread throughout the Near East, including Egypt, where the Greek dynasty of the Ptolemies ruled and where there were many Greek settlers, especially in Alexandria.

In polyglot communities like Alexandria, where Greeks, Egyptians, and Jews lived side by side, it was common for the script of one linguistic group to be applied to the languages of the other groups. This is what happened in Egypt, where the Greek alphabet came to be used for writing Egyptian and, on a smaller scale, for writing Hebrew, too.[3] The Greek letters did not have enough advantages over the Hebrew letters to threaten the latter with extinction. After all, the Hebrew script is alphabetic and with only twenty-two letters is a trifle easier to learn than the Greek alphabet of twenty-four letters. But Egyptian hieroglyphs were doomed to a slow death as soon as Egyptian began to be written in Greek letters. The old complex system could not compete with the new simple system.

[2] The art of the scribe was the first steppingstone on the way leading up to the highest positions in the Pharaoh's government. In principle, it was open to any boy who demonstrated diligence and capacity in his studies. In this regard, Egypt was democratic.

[3] Phoenician, Punic, and Eteocretan (which are closely related to Hebrew) are sometimes written in Greek letters. In the *Hexapla*, the Church Father Origen (*ca.* 185–254 A.D.) aligned two forms of the Hebrew Bible and four of its different Greek translations. He provided the Hebrew both in Hebrew letters and in Greek letters. It is tacitly assumed that Origen invented the idea of writing Hebrew texts in Greek letters, but it is more likely that the Hellenized Jews sometimes wrote Hebrew in Greek characters much as the Phoenicians, Carthaginians, and Eteocretans expressed their kindred Semitic dialects in Greek characters.

With the rise of Christianity in Egypt, the process whereby the Greek alphabet displaced the hieroglyphs for writing Egyptian was accelerated. Many of the early Christians were simple folk without any education in classical Egyptian. The Egyptian church adopted[4] the popular device of writing Scripture and other necessary texts in Greek letters but in the Egyptian language. Another factor played havoc with the very survival of hieroglyphic records: the latter were associated with paganism and frequently appeared in documents and on monuments depicting heathen gods. As a result, the early Church leaders in Egypt often stirred up their flock against the ancient relics and incited them to acts of vandalism.

The Coptic Church still preserves the native Egyptian language written in Greek characters, so that we have an unbroken tradition of Egyptian texts spanning about five thousand years.

With the passing of hieroglyphic writing in Roman times, erroneous ideas concerning its nature gained currency. The pronouncements of an Egyptian named Horapollo, who in late antiquity wrote a treatise called *Hieroglyphica*, carried particular weight in Europe from the High Renaissance down to the early decades of the nineteenth century. Some of his meanings of hieroglyphic signs are correct, but his fanciful explanations obscured the true nature of the system. The fallacy that persisted from late Roman times to the nineteenth century was that each Egyptian hieroglyph conveyed some mystical or spiritual idea.

If any people in all of recorded history (and I do not make

---

[4] There are a few pre-Christian Coptic texts (i.e., Egyptian texts in Greek letters), including incantations. Ignorant magicians often found it easier to inscribe spells alphabetically than in the more complicated Egyptian Hieroglyphic, Hieratic, or Demotic scripts.

an exception of the Americans) merits the description of "materialistic," it is the ancient Egyptians. They loved earthly life. Their cult of the dead is about as unspiritual as a religious concept can be. It aimed at achieving eternal life on a material plane. The body had to be preserved for a life full of the pleasures of this world with food, drink, servants, comforts, income, play, and games. No ancient Egyptian longed for a spiritual heaven with holy angels singing solemn hymns. We know from tomb paintings that the Egyptians aspired rather to pleasures such as a family boat trip on the Nile to catch fish and birds among the bulrushes, or a floor show of dancers and musicians. How such a fun-loving, materialistic people— whose character is revealed in their art as well as in the texts —came to be regarded as extraordinarily spiritual and mysterious illustrates how difficult it is for most people to take another culture on its own terms.

The "mysterious" Egyptians thus had a "mysterious" script full of mystical symbols ascribed to them. The decipherment of Hieroglyphic Egyptian required the replacement of the deep-seated notion of symbolism by the correct view that the main (though not the only) feature of the script is phonetic.

We may note at this juncture that while the decipherment of Egyptian has done away with the mysteries of the script, many people still regard the ancient Egyptians as a philosophical, mysterious folk whom we can never understand. Even the pyramids are sometimes thought to embody profound secrets that we mere mortals can never fathom. Actually, no accomplishment of the human race is less mysterious or more successful. The Egyptians lived in houses of perishable materials because they viewed earthly life as perishable. They regarded the after-life of men and the existence of the gods as enduring forever. Therefore, they purposely selected stone as the building material of eternity for permanent structures associated with religion and the cult of the dead. From less spectacular beginnings, they developed the great pyramids at Gizeh to endure for all time. No architects or builders have ever achieved their goal more efficiently and with such superb technique. Of all the Seven Wonders of antiquity, only the pyramids are still standing—marvels to behold. How the technological fulfilment of so clear an aim came to be regarded as mysterious shows how inflexible the corporate human mind can be. A rational approach would have us view the pyramid-builders as great engineers[5] rather than enigmatic mystery men of an inscrutable past.

A Jesuit professor of philosophy, mathematics, and oriental languages, Athanasius Kircher (1601–80), published in 1636 a study on Coptic in which he expressed his conviction that Coptic was a continuation of the ancient Egyptian language in alphabetic script. He was right, and the fact which he recognized was destined to provide the linguistic background for the decipherment of the hieroglyphs long afterward when the time was ripe.[6]

A few scholars in the eighteenth century suspected the existence of phonetic hieroglyphs and made the correct suggestion that the cartouche (an oval enclosing groups of signs) was used to contain the names of kings and queens. One of the savants who made this important observation was Johann Georg Zoëga, who published it in 1797. Then things began

[5] See L. Sprague de Camp, *The Ancient Engineers* (Norwalk, Conn.: Burndy Library, 1966), pp. 28–52.

[6] For Kircher's own account of his pioneer work on Coptic grammar and vocabulary, see C. W. Ceram, *Hands on the Past* (New York: Alfred A. Knopf, 1966), pp. 154–58. Though Kircher was mistaken about the nature of hieroglyphic writing, he understood the significance of Coptic as the linguistic key to the language of the hieroglyphs.

to move faster. In 1798 Napoleon invaded Egypt, and in 1799 a contingent of his expeditionary force discovered the Rosetta Stone, the key that started to unlock the secrets of the hieroglyphs.

The Rosetta Stone[7] is a black basalt slab that the French found in the course of rebuilding a fortification, in which it had already been reused as building material. The inscription that it bears in triplicate is a decree honoring the young pharaoh Ptolemy V Epiphanes in 196 B.C. The text enumerates his good deeds and rules that his statues and copies of this decree shall be set up in all the temples throughout Egypt. The three versions are in two languages but in three scripts— Hieroglyphic Egyptian, Demotic Egyptian, and Greek. In remote antiquity, a cursive form of the hieroglyphs had developed into a script called Hieratic. In late Pharaonic times, Hieratic was further simplified and stylized into Demotic. Under the Ptolemies, Greek became an important language in Egypt. Accordingly, in the closing centuries of the pre-Christian era, bilingual texts in Greek and Egyptian were written and provided the Greek key for deciphering the forgotten scripts of ancient Egypt.

Anglo-French strife affected the fate of the Rosetta Stone. A treaty forced its transfer to England, where it is still in the British Museum. A copy, made before the transfer, was delivered to the noted French orientalist Silvestre de Sacy. Though De Sacy did not make much headway with it, he showed it to the Swedish diplomat Johan David Åkerblad, who within two months made considerable progresss with the Demotic version. Åkerblad's *Lettre à M. de Sacy* (published in 1802) identified all the names occurring in the Demotic by

[7] E. A. Wallis Budge, *The Rosetta Stone* (London: British Museum, 1913), reprinted 1922 and 1927.

matching them with their counterparts in the Greek version and established the correct Demotic readings for "temples" and "Greeks" and the suffix meaning "he, him," or "his." Åkerblad rightly identified this suffix and these two nouns with their Coptic forms. (Though Demotic and Coptic are different in script, they are quite close linguistically.) After this remarkable start, Åkerblad was impeded from making further progress because of his erroneous idea that Demotic was exclusively alphabetic. The readings he figured out were indeed alphabetic, but much of Demotic writing is not alphabetic.

The Rosetta Stone is broken at the beginning (which contains the Hieroglyphic version) and to a lesser extent at the end (which contains the Greek translation). The Demotic, in the middle, while not intact, is the best preserved. Therefore, the earliest efforts at decipherment were aimed at the Demotic.

The next stride forward was made by an English physicist, Thomas Young, the author of the wave theory of light. Exemplifying the best in the culture of his era, he was also a doctor of medicine and wrote Latin with ease. Young was versatile as well as learned and had the kind of mind that is attracted to new and challenging problems. A copy of the Rosetta Stone fell into his hands in 1814. Young had benefited from the results of Åkerblad's work but realized that Demotic had so many signs that all of them could not possibly be alphabetic. He also sensed the relationship between the Hieroglyphic and Demotic systems. The repetitions in the Greek version enabled Young to break each of the three texts into their natural divisions and thereby to isolate the individual words. Soon he compiled a vocabulary of eighty-six Demotic words or word groups matched with their Greek translation; most are correct. However, the phonetic values he ascribed to the Demotic signs are not as a rule felicitous, and accordingly his Coptic cognates are generally mistaken. In 1816 he announced further discoveries made from texts other than the Rosetta Stone. He had matched long Hieroglyphic and Hieratic passages on papyri of the Book of the Dead, thus demonstrating the relationship between the pictorial and cursive forms of the writing. He proved (what others had previously suspected) that the cartouches enclosed royal names. In the papyri he noted variants in which certain signs could be replaced by other signs with the same phonetic values. Thus, Young established the principle of homophony. But Young's greatest contribution was his proof that the script was essentially phonetic and not philosophical, mystical, or symbolic.

Endowed with the spirit of a pioneer, Young was the first person to attempt the decipherment of the Hieroglyphic version of the Rosetta Stone. Assuming that the hieroglyphs for writing names of Greek origin had to be phonetic, he matched the opening seven signs in the recurring cartouche with *Ptolemaios* ("Ptolemy") in the Greek. The Egyptian scribes group those signs thus:

However, we shall string them out in a straight line and assign numbers to them:

By matching these signs with *Ptolemaios*, Young proposed the following phonetic values: $1 = p$, $2 = t$, 3 (zero value), $4 = ole$, $5 = ma$, $6 = i$, $7 = os$. We still render Nos. 1 and 2 the way Young did. He was wrong only about No. 3, which has the value o. He was partly right regarding the rest: 4 has the value l; we now transliterate 5 as m, 6 as y, and 7 as s.

On another monument, Young correctly identified the

cartouche ⟨ hieroglyphs ⟩ as "Berenice." To

simplify the decipherment, we set the signs in a straight line
and number them:

hieroglyph	hieroglyph	hieroglyph	hieroglyph	hieroglyph	hieroglyph	hieroglyph	hieroglyph
1	2	3	4	5	6	7	8

Young's identifications were basically correct, but to facilitate
matters, we shall assign the values we now know to be right:
$1 = b, 2 = r, 3 = n, 4 = y, 5 = k, 6 = $ ', $7 = t$,[8] $8 = $ (EGG
serving as determinative for feminine names).[9]

Young's demonstration that Egyptian writing is phonetic
may be considered the rudimentary foundation of scientific
Egyptology. His correct conclusions were inevitably mingled
with errors, but this does not diminish his achievement.

In 1815 J. W. Bankes excavated at Philae a granite obelisk
inscribed with a Hieroglyphic inscription on all four surfaces.
He also found nearby the base block on which it may possibly
have been set. The block, which carries three different but
related Greek inscriptions, names Ptolemy IX (Euergetes II)
and his wife, Cleopatra. None of the three Greek inscriptions
corresponds to the Hieroglyphic inscription.[10] Nevertheless,

[8] In older stages of the Egyptian language, the ending of feminine substan-
tives was –t. In later times, owing to a phonetic shift, the final –t was
dropped, though it continued to be written as historic spelling (compare the
French *doigt* "finger," which is pronounced *dwa*, but the g and t are written
historically, recalling the Latin origin of the word: *digitus*). Accordingly,
final –t, even though unpronounced, became a kind of graphic indicator of
feminine names (including foreign ones like Berenice and Cleopatra).

[9] In effect we have two feminine determinatives (the –t and the EGG) without
any phonetic value here.

[10] E. A. Wallis Budge, *The Decrees of Memphis and Canopus* (London: Ke-
gan Paul, Trench, Trübner, 1904), 3 vols.; see I, 135–59, for the Greek and
Hieroglyphic inscriptions on the Philae obelisk and base block.

the Hieroglyphic inscription includes a pair of cartouches, the first of which contains "Ptolemy" as inscribed on the Rosetta Stone. In 1818 Bankes rightly took the other cartouche to contain the name of Cleopatra. The cartouche appears thus:

. We shall number the signs as

follows:

From the values established through the decipherment of the cartouches of Ptolemy and Berenice, we know that $2 = l$, $4 = o$, $5 = p$, $8 = r$, while 10, which is the t sign, appears here only because the name is feminine and 11 is the determinative for feminine names. Accordingly, we have the following skeleton: $(1)L(3)OP(6)(7)R(9)$, and since the name is "Kleopatra," $1 = k$, $3 = e$, and 6 and $9 = a$. There is an apparent problem concerning 7, which must equal t, even though a different letter for t occurs as the second sign in the name "Ptolemy." Here we are confronted with the problem of homophony: different signs standing for the same sound.

In January, 1822, the text with Bankes's identification was transmitted to Champollion, who soon afterwards made use of it in his decipherment of Egyptian. Unfortunately, the question of priority in such matters is a touchy subject, and we have anticipated the detailed decipherment of Cleopatra's name in order to stress Bankes's important identification made before the great breakthrough by Champollion, later in 1822.

The Frenchman destined to go far beyond Young's Egyptological discoveries was Jean François Champollion, born at Figeac, in the Department du Lot, on December 23, 1790. He was a child prodigy who, at the age of eleven, decided that he would decipher the Hieroglyphic inscriptions. By his twelfth year he had begun the study of Hebrew and Arabic. As a teen-ager in Grenoble he studied ancient history, Coptic, and various scripts that might someday help him reveal the secrets of the Rosetta Stone. He became professor of history at the Lyceum of Grenoble at the age of eighteen. For political reasons he lost a series of posts and in 1820 found refuge with his older brother, Jacques Joseph Champollion-Figeac, an archeologist, who ever encouraged Jean François during the latter's life and subsequently edited his posthumous publications.

So strong was Jean François's dedication to his Egyptological dream that he continued his Egyptian and Coptic studies unflaggingly during those stormy years. Equipped with a thorough knowledge of Coptic and Egyptian history, he was ready to make his epochal contributions. Thanks to his study of the Rosetta Stone and numerous other Egyptian inscriptions, he was able (in a brochure published in 1821) to transpose a Demotic or Hieratic or Hieroglyphic text into either of the other two. New texts were turning up, and there was enough source material to go ahead.

It is interesting to note that the outstanding orientalist of France, A. I. Silvestre de Sacy (1758–1838), tried to dissuade Champollion from attempting to decipher Hieroglyphic Egyptian and conceived a dislike for the student who was to eclipse him.[11] De Sacy, who was generous in such matters to Åkerblad and Young, lost no love on the most promising student

[11] *Ibid.*, p. 115 (for De Sacy's attempt to dissuade Champollion from attempting to decipher Egyptian) and pp. 68 and 70–71 (for De Sacy's denigration of Champollion's ability and intellectual honesty). On the surface, however, De Sacy and Champollion kept up appearances, so that in Champollion's hour of triumph, the younger man could pay open tribute to the elder, who in turn could reciprocate with accolades in public.

he ever met. De Sacy was not only learned; he was also accomplished, but he lacked the qualities that a pioneer must
have for scoring any primary breakthrough, and was not big
enough to encourage them in one of his own students.

Until nearly the end of 1821 Champollion did not extricate
himself from the fallacy that the hieroglyphs were symbolic.
So deeply ingrained was this error that he thought the lion
(which merely stands for the letter *l*) in Ptolemy's cartouche
symbolized war because *p(t)olemos* (the root of Ptolemy's
name) is the Greek word for "war." At long last, on December
21, 1821, he abandoned the false notion of symbolism and
concluded that the script must have phonetic signs. He realized this from a simple count, which showed that there are
about three times as many hieroglyphs as words in the Greek
and therefore the hieroglyphs must include phonetic signs.
He soon identified a number of Greek and Latin names and
titles in their Hieroglyphic transcription, which enabled him
to enlarge the list of phonetic values. Let us examine a few of
them to see how the work was done:

The cartouche has these

signs:

From the cartouches of Ptolemy, Berenice, and Cleopatra,
we know that 1 = *a*, 2 = *l*, 4 = *s*, 5 = a vowel like *e*, 6 = *n*,
7 = *t*, and 8 = *r*. The skeleton of the name is Al–sentr–,
which Champollion identified with "Alexander" in its Greek
form "Aleksandros." Therefore, 3 = *k*, 5 = *a* (even though
it corresponds to *e* elsewhere), and 7 = *d* (though it corre-

sponds to Greek *t* elsewhere), while 9 was another *s* (in accordance with the homophonous nature of the script).

The cartouche was now quite simple to identify.

= *kysrs* = Kaisaros, the Greek form of "Caesar."

The cartouche containing

could now be read (*a*) (2) (*t/d*) (4) (*k/g*) (*l/r*) (*t/d*) (*l/r*). Since 2 and 4 are the same sign, Champollion correctly identified this group as *autokrator* (the Greek royal title) with 2 and 4 representing *w/u/o*.

Identifying with Hadrian(os), we have

	1	2	3	4	5	6
		t/d	*r*		*n*	*s*

Champollion saw that 1 = *h* and 4 = some sound like *ia*.

In texts of the Ptolemaic and Roman periods, Champollion also identified the Hieroglyphic form of the royal Greek title Sebastos and of the names of Roman emperors such as Tiberius, Domitian, Trajan, and Antoninus as well as of Germanicus. But all the decipherment was so far limited to the final stage of Hieroglyphic writing in Greco-Roman times.

Until September, 1822, Champollion still felt that perhaps only foreign names and titles were written phonetically. How were the native names of the old Pharaohs written? It was on September 14, 1822, that he succeeded in answering this question. Now that he could pronounce at least some of the signs, he turned to cartouches from the older periods, long before the Greeks and Romans. Thus, he noted ⊙ 𓇓 𓏤 𓏤

in a cartouche from a rock temple at Abu Simbel. The last two signs he could read as -ss and the circle he identified as the "sun," which is pronounced re in Coptic. Could the series Re–ss stand for Ramses? All doubts were dispelled when he

turned to another cartouche (𓅝 𓇓 𓏤) with the ibis

of Thoth, so that this Pharaonic name could only be Thothmes.

Then in the Rosetta Stone Champollion noted that 𓇓 𓏤

occurred in a group corresponding to genethlia "birthday celebrations" in the Greek, tying in with Coptic misi, mose "to give birth." The battle was won. The phonetic system was clear, and the linguistic relationship of Hieroglyphic and Coptic Egyptian was established. From that day on, progress was assured, and the present stage of Egyptology—with all its great corpora of texts, dictionaries, grammars, histories, and innumerable special studies—was only a matter of time and labor.

On September 27, 1822, Champollion notified the Academy of Paris that he had succeeded in deciphering Egyptian, in his famous Lettre à M. Dacier relative à l'alphabet des hiéroglyphes phonétiques. He read the letter before the Academy on September 29 but omitted many of his most important observations, including his identification of the names of Ramses and Thothmes. These and many other points were first published in his remarkable *Précis du système hiérogly-phique*, which appeared in 1824.

Much of the rest of his short life was spent gathering and studying material in Italy and Egypt. When he died on March 4, 1832, at the age of forty-one, he had established the character of Egyptian writing (differentiating ideograms, phonograms, and phonetic complements), the relationship between Pharaonic Egyptian and Coptic, and the foundations of Egyptian grammar and lexicography. Though he started with bilinguals, he eventually succeeded in translating unilinguals. His achievement is now self-evident, but for many years after his death his claims continued to be contested.

"Champollion's brilliant discoveries met with great opposition, much of it acrimonious and personal, chiefly from scholars reared in the classical tradition, who resented the prominence given by these discoveries to an ancient 'barbarian' nation."[12] Scholars belong to guilds held together by common opinions, attitudes, and methods. As a rule, innovation is welcome only when it is confined to surface details and does not modify the structure as a whole. For this reason, new interpretations of a problematic word or verse may be applauded by the very academicians who will stop at nothing to discredit a breakthrough destined to touch off a major reappraisal of the entire field. The academic tradition still produces a plethora of obstructionists to oppose any major advance that involves the contribution of "barbarians" like the Egyptians or Semites to the Mediterranean civilization underlying Greece and Rome. How incapable these obstructionists are of appreciating the real spirit of classical literature is all too evident. A great Greek, Herodotus, clearly perceived

[12] *Encyclopaedia Britannica* (1964), "Champollion."

the indebtedness of Greece to ancient Egypt, but his spirit has not yet penetrated the minds of many who teach his *History*. Constructive criticism is still needed in Egyptology; it was needed even more in Champollion's finest hour. But destructive denigration is an unworthy characteristic of academia, and it is directed with most virulence against those who are in the forefront of progress.

The opposition to Champollion's decipherment came to an end in 1866 when a bilingual stela, in Hieroglyphic and Demotic Egyptian and Greek, was discovered and published by a group of German scholars, including Richard Lepsius (who more than any other person marked the transition from the pioneering stage to the age of refinement in Egyptology). The text, known as the Decree of Canopus,[13] is the same kind of inscription as the Rosetta Stone (the latter is sometimes called the Decree of Memphis). In 238 B.C. the priests, assembled at Canopus, promulgated the Decree, in which they enumerated the beneficent deeds of Ptolemy III and his wife Berenice and provided for honoring both of them and their ancestors. At the same time they established every fourth year as a leap year with an extra day. The style of the Decree of Canopus shed considerable light on the style of the Rosetta Stone, which was written in the same tradition over forty years later. The long and almost perfectly preserved Decree of Canopus confirmed Champollion's decipherment and added further source material to the rapidly growing field of Egyptology. Champollion's battle for acceptance was won, but not until the hero had been dead for thirty-four years.[14]

[13] Budge, *Decrees of Memphis and Canopus*, III, 1–201.
[14] We should not paint a completely gloomy picture of Champollion's struggle. He had friends as well as foes and lived to enjoy some recognition. He was made a Chevalier of the Legion of Honor and eventually, after great opposition, Professor of Egyptology at the Collège de France.

His fame remains secure, while his detractors have gone to their well-earned oblivion.

The sequel is important but in the context of this book need not be dealt with at length. Adolph Erman guided Egyptology in the direction of its present status. He wrote a fine study of Late Egyptian (i.e., the language after Ikhnaton in the fourteenth century B.C.), initiated the great Berlin dictionary of the Egyptian language, produced the standard work on life in ancient Egypt, and trained a generation of scholars who brought still greater finesse to Egyptology. The standard textbook is Alan Gardiner's *Egyptian Grammar*,[15] an amazing work in more ways than one. The author set out to compose a beginner's book with graduated exercises from Egyptian to English and from English to Egyptian. It is divided into lessons with grammatical topics illustrated profusely with selections from the whole range of the literature. The vocabularies are valuable, but the exhaustive and annotated sign list is indispensable. What began as an elementary textbook ended up as the Bible of Egyptology. Studying Gardiner's *Grammar* is the foundation for a career in Egyptian; no scholar, no matter how advanced, ever outgrows his need of it.

Egyptian history is a vast subject in itself. Perhaps the best treatment is to be found in *L'Égypte* by E. Drioton and J. Vandier.[16] But an earlier treatment is in a way more important: Egypt is covered in E. Meyer's *Geschichte des Altertums*[17] (i.e., *History of Antiquity*), which also embraces Mesopotamia, Israel, Iran, Anatolia, and Greece. Meyer had a breadth of knowledge that is becoming more and more rare in an age of specialization. He not only knew the histories of the in-

---

[15] New York: Oxford University Press, 3rd ed., 1957.
[16] Paris: Presses Universitaires de France, 4th ed., 1962.
[17] Stuttgart: J. G. Gotta'sche Buchhandlung, 2nd ed., 1907–37, 3 vols.

dividual nations, but perceived their relationships. Egypt is of great interest in its own right, but its importance lies in its impact on the origins and development of Western civilization. Moreover, the decipherment of Egyptian had an effect on the decipherment of the other scripts and languages that we are about to follow.

Before taking leave of Egyptian, it will be of interest to look at a Hieroglyphic text with its transliteration and translation. The selection is extracted from a stela of Sesostris III[18] and reflects the vigor that made Egypt great:

ir gr m-ḫt pḥ
He who desists after attack

sšm ib pw n ḫryw
is a strengthener of the enemy's heart.

qnt pw 'd
To be aggressive is brave

[18] Gardiner, *Egyptian Grammar*, p. 361.

ḫst pw ḥm-ḫt
to retreat is cowardice.

ḥm pw mᶜ ᵓrw ḥr tᵓš.f
A real poltroon is he who is debarred from his own frontier

dr-ntt sdm Nḥs r ḥr n r
the Nubian hears so that he falls at a word

ỉn wšb.f dd ḥm.f
answering him causes him to retreat.

ᵓd.t(w) r.f
If one is aggressive toward him

dd.f sᵓ.f
he gives his back

ḥm-ḫt.(tw)
If one retreats

w'.f r 'd
he falls into aggression.

n rmṯ(t) ỉs nt šft st
They are not people of worth

ḫwrw pw sḏw ỉbw
they are cowards broken of heart.

3

GROTEFEND'S
DECIPHERMENT
OF OLD PERSIAN

The same intellectual climate in Europe that led to the decipherment of Egyptian simultaneously produced the decipherment of cuneiform. In 1802, the very year that Åkerblad scored his success in reading parts of the Demotic version of the Rosetta Stone, a young German high school teacher cracked the system of Old Persian Cuneiform.

"Cuneiform" is not one script, but a variety of different

systems of writing with wedge-shaped signs (for the Latin word for "wedge, nail" is *cuneus*). Cuneiform was developed by writing on soft clay with a stylus that ended in a triangle, whence the triangular nail-head on all of the component parts of the signs. For certain kinds of texts, such as royal inscriptions on mountain walls, the scribes incised the signs with chisels. On neither soft nor hard materials did cuneiform lose its wedge-and-line character. To the end it shunned curves and never went through any stylistic transformation of the kind we see in the development of Hieroglyphic into Hieratic and finally into Demotic. During its three thousand years of history, the cuneiform signs became simplified and were formed with fewer wedges, but they never became cursive.

The earliest important language expressed in cuneiform was Sumerian, with both ideographic and phonetic signs, along with determinatives and phonetic complements much like Egyptian. The Semites of Mesopotamia, who are called the Akkadians, borrowed Sumerian writing to express their own Akkadian language. Later, other nations, such as Elamites, Hurrians, Hittites, and Urarteans, took over the same script from the Akkadians to write their own languages. But the Persians during the Achaemenian dynasty (sixth to fourth centuries B.C.)[1] devised a simplified system of writing using fewer than forty alphabetic and syllabic signs plus half a dozen ideograms. This Old Persian resembles Sumero-Akkadian writing only insofar as both are cuneiform; no sign in the one can be pronounced or translated on the basis of any similar sign in the other.

At a number of Persian and Median sites, trilingual inscriptions on stone buildings and on mountain walls attracted the

[1] For the historic background of ancient nations discussed in this book, see C. H. Gordon, *The Ancient Near East* (New York: Norton, 1965).

attention of European travelers. All three versions are in cuneiform, but unlike the trigraphic Rosetta Stone, none of the three cuneiform scripts could be read. Accordingly, the decipherers of cuneiform had to undertake, so to speak, the solution of an equation with three unknowns and no knowns. It is therefore necessary for us to trace the rediscovery of the essential elements of information that led to the decipherment of Old Persian Cuneiform in 1802, which in turn made it possible to decipher Sumero-Akkadian Cuneiform and push back history in western Asia by two millennia.

There are not as many references in ancient Greek literature to cuneiform as there are to Egyptian hieroglyphs. Herodotus,[2] however, states that Darius set up two columns at the Bosphorus—one with Assyrian letters, one with Greek letters. The *grammata assyria* ("Assyrian letters") of Herodotus can only mean cuneiform. But for all intents and purposes the very existence of cuneiform was forgotten in the mainstream of European culture.

In the Age of Discovery that followed the Renaissance, a succession of Europeans began to visit the Persian sites where the Achaemenian and later Persian rulers left inscriptions and sculptures in the living rock. In 1472 Giosafat Barbaro was dispatched to Persia as the Venetian ambassador. He visited Persepolis (the capital built mainly by Darius and Xerxes),[3] the nearby site of Naqsh-e-Rustam (a veritable outdoor museum of Achaemenian and Middle Persian antiquities), and the earlier Achaemenian capital of Pasargade, where Cyrus the Great had ruled. It was not until 1545, however, that Barbaro's *Viagi fatti da Vinetia alla Tana* was published.

[2] *History*, 4:87.
[3] In this book "Darius" (521–485 B.C.) and "Xerxes" (485–465 B.C.) always refer to "the First" kings of those names.

The first European to write about the cuneiform inscriptions was Pietro della Valle, who discussed them in a letter sent from Shiraz in 1621 to a friend in Naples. The letter includes his copy of five Old Persian Cuneiform signs.

Jean Chardin (1643–1713) visited Persepolis and other sites in 1666, 1667, and 1674, although his *Voyages* (published in Amsterdam) did not appear until 1711. He opposed the common view that cuneiform was not writing at all but simply decoration. Chardin was the first modern author to study the inscriptions carefully, to publish a complete text in all three versions (Old Persian, Elamite, and Babylonian), and to provide a good description of the Naqsh-e-Rustam texts. He decided, correctly, that cuneiform goes from left to right.

Engelbert Kämpfer (1651–1716), who visited Persepolis in 1686, described the signs as "*cuneatae*" (i.e., "cuneiform"), thus giving the script the name by which it is now known.

The man who made enough source material available for the decipherment of Old Persian was Carsten Niebuhr (1733–1815) from Danish Holstein. He was first drawn toward the study of mathematics, but he also devoted himself to Arabic. That language helped qualify him to join the expedition sent by Frederic V of Denmark in 1761 to explore Arabia. This assignment enabled him to travel in Egypt, Syria, Palestine, and Arabia as far south as Sanaa. In 1762 and 1763 several members of the expedition died. In 1764, Niebuhr and the expedition surgeon sailed for Bombay. During the voyage the surgeon died, leaving Niebuhr as the only survivor of the expedition. After spending fourteen months in Bombay, Niebuhr set out on a series of travels in Persia and Mesopotamia. Early in March, 1765, he went to Persepolis, where he spent three weeks surveying the site, making ground plans of the buildings, and copying inscriptions. It was his clear copies that made the decipherment possible. In 1788 he published correct and complete copies of several important trilinguals of Darius and Xerxes, some long and some published for the first time. He recognized that three different systems of writing were involved.

In 1798, Olav Gerhard Tychsen (1734–1813), an orientalist from Rostock, was the first to make use of Niebuhr's copies. He recognized that a divider separated words in the first system (which we now know to be the Old Persian), and correctly assumed that the systems of writing expressed three different languages.

In 1802 a Danish scholar, Friedrich Münter (1761–1830), correctly ascribed the trilinguals to the Achaemenian kings. He independently recognized the word-divider in the first version and suggested it was alphabetic, while the second version was syllabic and the third ideographic. While not entirely correct, this observation was, on all three counts, a step in the right direction. Münter deduced from the parallel repetitions in the three versions that all three dealt with the same subject matter. He also spotted the signs designating "king" and "king of kings."

The successful and complete decipherment of Old Persian required the knowledge of some closely related language. We have seen how Coptic provided the linguistic data required for the recovery of the old Egyptian language. But the situation in Iran was not the same as in Egypt, where the native Coptic Church still preserves the Egyptian language in Greek letters. When Alexander the Great destroyed the Achaemenian Empire (331-330 B.C.), Achaemenian civilization—script and all—was doomed. Later, when the Parthians and Sasanians ruled Iran, they wrote the Persian language in letters derived from the Aramaic alphabet. It is true that the Zoroastrians of Iran preserved very ancient Persian writings, the Zend-Avesta, but with the Arab conquest, the Iranians were steadily converted to Islam, so that today there is only a tiny (but respected) Zoroastrian minority in Iran. The Zoroastrians who fled to India are now called the Parsees, a prosperous and educated minority that has retained its identity and perpetuated a knowledge of the ancient Zoroastrian scriptures in Persian. The situation required that European scholars master the Zend-Avesta from Parsee teachers in India and make that language available to the orientalists who would some day elucidate the Old Persian Cuneiform inscriptions.

Abraham Hyacinthe Anquetil-Duperron (1731–1801) went to India, where he studied Persian under Parsee teachers and prepared a translation of the Zend-Avesta. On returning to France, he revised and published the translation in 1771, incidentally providing the linguistic basis for getting at the Old Persian Cuneiform texts.

The towering figure in oriental studies was Silvestre de Sacy, who played a role, as we have seen, in the beginnings of Egyptology. In 1793 he published his *Mémoires sur diverses Antiquités de Perse*, in which he published some short Pehlevi (Middle Persian) inscriptions of the Sasanian kings at Naqsh-e-Rustam. By using the Greek version of bilinguals, he was able to decipher the Pehlevi original in which the king would call himself "A., the great king, the king of kings, the king of Iran and non-Iran, the son of B., the great king. . . ." We may now turn to the pioneer who used this and other collateral information to score the breakthrough.

Georg Friedrich Grotefend (1775–1853), a high school teacher in Göttingen, loved to solve cryptograms. In 1802, when the challenge of deciphering ancient scripts was very much in the cultural atmosphere, Grotefend tried his hand at Old Persian. Although he was not an orientalist, he had studied philology and had the knack of ferreting out the essential collateral information required for solving problems.

Inspired by De Sacy's translation of the royal Pehlevi formulas, Grotefend assumed that the latter followed an Old Persian tradition. He had correctly decided that the first version of the trilinguals should be in the native language of the Achaemenian kings. The Old Persian signary, which has fewer different signs than the other two, requires more signs to write the same text than the other two systems. In fact, there are sometimes as many as ten signs between word-dividers in the Old Persian. All this led Grotefend to guess that the script was alphabetic (for it is more likely that words have ten alphabetic letters than ten syllables). Actually the Old Persian system is a compromise between an alphabet and a syllabary, but Grotefend was close enough to the truth to achieve a notable measure of success by comparing two different but typologically related inscriptions published by Niebuhr. The relation was clear to Grotefend from the recurrence of words and phrases in the same sequence. To bring this out, we shall align the two texts in parallel columns and indent the words that are identical in both texts:

The transliteration and translation of both texts will help the reader follow Grotefend's reasoning:

TEXT 1

1) *da-a-ra-ya-va-u-sha*
   Darius

2) *kha-sha-a-ya-tha-i-ya*
   king

3) *va-za-ra-ka*
   great

4) *kha-sha-a-ya-tha-i-ya*
   king

5) *kha-sha-a-ya-tha-i-ya-a-*
   na-a-ma
   of kings

6) *kha-sha-a-ya-tha-i-ya*
   king

7) *da-ba-ya-u-na-a-ma*
   of countries

TEXT 2

kha-sha-ya-a-ra-sha-a
Xerxes

kha-sha-a-ya-tha-i-ya
king

va-za-ra-ka
great

kha-sha-a-ya-tha-i-ya
king

kha-sha-a-ya-tha-i-ya-a-
na-a-ma
of kings

TEXT 1

8) *vi-i-sha-ta-a-sa-pa-ha-ya-a*
of Hystaspes

9)

10) *pa-u-ca*
son

11) *ha-kha-a-ma-na-i-sha-*
i-ya
Achaemenian

12) *ha-ya*
who

13) *i-ma-ma*
this

14) *ta-ca-ra-ma*
palace

15) *a-ku-u-na-u-sha*
built.

TEXT 2

da-a-ra-ya-va-ha-u-sha
of Darius
kha-sha-a-ya-tha-i-ya-ha-ya-a
of king

pa-u-ca
son
ha-kha-a-ma-na-i-sha-i-ya

Achaemenian.

In normal English these texts are to be translated:

Darius, the great king, the king of kings, the king of countries, the son of Hystaspes, the Achaemenian, (is the one) who built this palace.

Xerxes, the great king, the king of kings, the son of King Darius, the Achaemenian.

Applying the Sasanian formula ("A., the great king, the king of kings, the king of Iran and non-Iran, the son of B., the great king, . . ."), Grotefend saw in line 1 the name of the respective king and in lines 2–5 his title "great king, king of kings." Accordingly, in lines 2, 4, and 5 there is the word for "king"; the longer form in line 5 should contain the suffix of the genitive plural ("of kings"). The word in line 10 should mean "son," for the formula requires the king's paternity. Since in text 2 the word for "king" occurs in line 9 (just before "son"), line 8 must contain the name of the king's father. In text 2, the king's father is none other than the king (genitive) whose name appears as the king (nominative) in the first line of text 1. But the name of the latter's father (text 1, line 8) is not followed by the title "king." Therefore, text 2 was written for the son of the king for whom text 1 was written. But the king in text 1 was not the son of a king. Who could the king in text 2 be?

Grotefend decided on King Xerxes, son of King Darius, son of Hystaspes (for Hystaspes is never given the title of king by Herodotus). This conclusion is supported by the fact that "Darius" and "Xerxes" are of about the same length (six letters in Greek, seven in Old Persian), while "Hystaspes" is longer (nine in Greek, ten in the O.P. genitive). Therefore, text 1:1 contains the name "Darius" in the nominative and text 2:8 contains the same name in the genitive, while text 2:1 contains "Xerxes" in the nominative. Text 1:8 thus contains the genitive form of the name of Darius's father Hystaspes, who was not a king.

By operating with what he considered to be the Old Persian forms of Hystaspes, Darius, and Xerxes and by assuming that the script was an alphabet, Grotefend got the following phonetic values, which we shall compare with the transliteration currently used:

NAME	GROTEFEND'S TRANSLITERATION	CORRECT TRANSLITERATION
Hystaspes	*g o sh t a s p*	v^i *i* sh^a t^a *a* s^a p^a
Darius	*d a r h e u sh*	d^a *a* r^a y^a v^a *u* sh^a
Xerxes	*kh sh h a r sh a*	kh^a sh^a y^a *a* r^a sh^a *a*

The "correct" (i.e., correct in the sense that it is now accepted) transliteration reckons with inherent vowels, which may or may not be disregarded in the pronunciation. When they are disregarded, the signs are used alphabetically, as Grotefend assumed. Grotefend's absolutely alphabetic transliteration is no further from the correct one than our absolutely syllabic transliteration, and we should not consider it an error, especially in the work of the pioneer. Accordingly, from those three names alone he got the right phonetic values for *sh, t, a, s, p, d, r, u, kh*: nine signs, thus laying the foundation for reading the Old Persian inscriptions. He also identified the words for "king" and "great," and later, in 1815, he identified the name of "Cyrus" in an inscription from Murghab. This he was able to do after a British diplomat who knew Persia well, James Justinian Morier (1780–1849), identified the tomb at Murghab as Cyrus's. The native Persians had lost all memory of Cyrus, who had made of them the world's greatest power, and they attributed his tomb to Madar-e-Suleiman (the mother of King Solomon).

Grotefend's task was more difficult than the decipherment of Egyptian, where an intelligible Greek translation provided the key. The decipherment of Old Persian was the work of a genius who sniffed out the few essential texts and facts to solve with directness and economy of material and time a problem that seemed incapable of a solution.

On September 4, 1802, Grotefend presented his paper with the solution to the Göttingen Academy. The Academy did not consider it worth publishing and printed only a short notice about it. Silvestre de Sacy displayed more intelligence by writing up a full account of Grotefend's decipherment, including both of the Old Persian texts complete with transliteration and translation, for Millin's *Magasin Encyclopédique* (1803). Another detailed report was published in Arnold Heeren's rather broad study, *Ideen über die Politik, den Verkehr und den Handel der vornehmsten Völker der alten Welt*.[4] But in general Grotefend's decipherment was disregarded by the orientalists, who should have recognized its importance and built upon it.

Bilingual confirmation of Grotefend's decipherment was pointed out in 1823 by J. A. Saint Martin (1791–1832) on a vase that had been published in 1762 by Count Caylus. The vase bears a quadrilingual inscription in Old Persian, Elamite, Babylonian, and Hieroglyphic Egyptian. Champollion had read the Egyptian. The text says, "Xerxes, the Great King," every word of which had been read by Grotefend on the

---

[4] *Ideas on the Politics, Relations and Trade of the Leading Peoples of Antiquity.*

Persepolis inscriptions in 1802. But this bilingual confirmation of the decipherments of Old Persian and Egyptian did not dispel the misgivings or indifference of the run-of-the-mill specialists who so often on such occasions are too obtuse to know that something highly significant has happened in their own field.

Forty years after Grotefend's death, the world of learning made amends to the pioneer. In 1893 his manuscript was recovered and published in full, a landmark in the history of cuneiform studies. The refusal of the Göttingen Academy to publish it nine decades earlier is unfortunately not a unique act of stupidity. Academies, committees, editorial boards and the like are usually composed of men who are "down to earth." To them the work of genius may be indistinguishable from folly.

In identifying the sounds of twelve Old Persian signs (i.e., a third of the phonetic symbols), Grotefend had laid the foundation of the decipherment. The reason he could not make more headway was twofold. First, he had no access to the great trilingual of Darius at Behistun. Secondly, he was not enough of an orientalist to master the growing field of ancient Persian studies. The completion of the task of deciphering Old Persian required a knowledge of the Zend-Avesta and the related Sanskrit language. The nascent discipline of Indo-Iranian linguistics had an important contribution to make.

Rasmus Christian Rask (1787–1832), a Danish authority on Zend and Pehlevi, studied Grotefend's decipherment and concluded that the language of the Achaemenian inscriptions was closely related to Zend Persian, both coming from approximately the same age. In 1826 Rask read correctly the genitive plural suffix *-ānām* occurring in the phrase "king of kings" and thereby established the right values for the *na* and *ma* signs.

In 1836 the Zend scholar Eugène Burnouf (1801–1852) published his *Mémoire sur deux inscriptions cunéiformes*, in which he succeeded in identifying two more signs correctly. His knowledge of Zend and Sanskrit enabled him to translate several Old Persian words, of which the most important and useful was *a-da-ma* (*adam*) "I (am)." Burnouf realized the importance of the Zend-Avesta for Old Persian studies, and when his commentary on the Yaçna (a liturgical work that forms the third part of the Avesta) appeared in 1834, its value was recognized by the scholars in Europe engaged in the decipherment of the Old Persian inscriptions.

In the same year (1836) that Burnouf's *Mémoire* was published, Christian Lassen (1800–1876) published *Die altpersischen Keilinschriften*, which covered much of the same ground as Burnouf. Both scholars happened to be friends and were in touch with each other. But Lassen had a good idea which produced outstanding results. Remembering that Herodotus[5] tells us that Darius inscribed the names of the nations that made up his armed forces upon the pillars he set up by the Bosphorus, Lassen thought such a list ought to appear among the Persepolis texts. He found one that mentioned twenty-four proper names, of which he identified nineteen. This enabled him to increase the number of signs with known phonetic values to twenty-three. Knowing the Avestan forms of the names was of prime value to Lassen. From his command of Sanskrit, he recognized that in Old Persian (as in Sanskrit writing), short *a* was not written after the normal series of consonants. That is, what Grotefend read as *t, d, r, kh, sh, s*, etc., may also

[5] *History* 4:87.

stand for *ta, da, ra, kha, sha, sa,* etc. The *a* sign follows only to indicate long *ā;* e.g., *da-a* stands for *dā.*

In 1837 E. E. F. Beer (1805–1841) identified two more signs, while Eugène Vincent Stanislas Jacquet (1811–1838) identified six (including the two independently found by Beer). Although these two men were not able to improve on the translations of Burnouf and Lassen, the new values they found helped Iranologists add to the vocabulary of Old Persian.[6]

The importance of the decipherment of Old Persian goes far beyond the limited corpus of the Achaemenian inscriptions in the Persian language. Through the phonetic evidence of the proper names, the Elamite and Akkadian versions were deciphered in the trilinguals. Once Akkadian was deciphered, it opened up the vast literatures in Akkadian and Sumerian from Babylonia, Assyria, and the entire Near East. And it was only a matter of time for the unlocking of Hittite and other literatures written in the Akkadian system of cuneiform. As a result, our historical and philological knowledge has been widened enormously.

Grotefend's decipherment was destined to be eclipsed by the work of a different kind of pioneer, Rawlinson, about whom we shall read in the next chapter. But Grotefend's achievement stands out as a gem of brilliant simplicity. Great thinking is often direct and naïve. Such was Grotefend's decipherment in 1802.

[6] Many of the details concerning the decipherment of cuneiform are covered by E. A. Wallis Budge, *The Rise and Progress of Assyriology* (London: Martin Hopkinson & Co., 1925). A brief account is given by David Kahn, *The Codebreakers* (New York: Macmillan, 1967), pp. 912–14.

4

RECLAIMING THE
SUMERO-AKKADIAN
LEGACY

The towering giant among the pioneers in cuneiform studies is the Englishman Henry Creswicke Rawlinson (1810–1895). During his school days at Ealing, he was especially interested in the Greek and Latin historians. At the same time, he was good in athletics. His intellectual and physical abilities combined to equip him for the great task that lay ahead. In 1827 he was sent by the East India Company to India, where he studied Persian, Arabic, and

Hindustani and gained enough proficiency to become the interpreter as well as paymaster of the First Bombay Grenadiers in 1828. In 1835 he was selected for service in Iran as military adviser to the Shah's brother, who was governor of the province that included Kirmanshah (in Iranian Kurdistan).

Though Rawlinson may have heard about what Grotefend and other scholars had achieved in Europe, there is no reason to suspect that he had any specific information about the readings of any signs in any of the Old Persian inscriptions until the close of 1836. His indebtedness to his predecessors is in the nature of "stimulus diffusion" rather than of outright borrowing.

On his way to Kirmanshah he heard about two cuneiform inscriptions on Mount Elvend, near Hamadan. The natives still call the texts "Ganj Nameh" ("Treasure Story") because of the tradition that they tell where treasure is hidden. From these two inscriptions, which he copied in 1835 and checked in 1836, he concluded that one had been written for Darius, son of Hystaspes, and the other for Xerxes, son of Darius, and arrived at much the same results that Grotefend had long before, by treating similar material along similar lines.

After arriving in Kirmanshah, Rawlinson heard about the huge inscription with reliefs on the mountain wall at Behistun, about twenty-two miles east of the city. He visited the site often in 1835 and began to copy the text. Toward the close of 1836, he learned from Colonel Taylor, the British Resident in Baghdad, of Grotefend's accomplishment in deciphering Old Persian. But Rawlinson stated that Grotefend's values were of no use to him, because he himself had already identified more signs than Grotefend. In any case, Rawlinson's claim to fame is not for making the first decisive steps in the decipherment, for Grotefend anticipated him by a third of a

century. Rawlinson's great achievement hinges on his redis-
covering, copying, and deciphering the Behistun inscription,
which is longer and more important than all the other
Achaemenian trilinguals combined. At risk of life and limb,
Rawlinson spent years in copying the text and then used it
not only for the Old Persian but also for deciphering the most
important of the versions, the Babylonian. Moreover, he did
not keep all the material for himself but let others share in
the decipherment. The text tells how Darius quelled rebellions
at home and abroad and proclaims the might and extent of the
Empire. It is full of personal and geographical names that provided Rawlinson with the phonetic values of the signs. It also
contains plenty of narrative that revealed the grammar and
basic vocabulary of Old Persian.

In 1836 and 1837 Rawlinson succeeded in translating the
first two columns of the Old Persian section of the Behistun
inscription, totaling nearly 200 lines. He wrote up his account
of the text with transliteration, translation, and notes for the
Royal Asiatic Society in 1837. It reached London early in
1838. Edwin Norris (1795–1872) sent a copy of it to the
Société Asiatique in Paris so that Burnouf and other French
scholars might read it. They were so impressed that they
elected Rawlinson an honorary member of the Société and
sent him Burnouf's *Mémoire* of 1836 and book on the Yaçna
of 1833. It was on his paper of 1837, together with a supplement written in 1839, that Rawlinson based his claim of virtually completing the decipherment of the Old Persian script
and not, as is sometimes stated, on his fuller "Memoir."[1]

By identifying the names of Hystaspes, Darius, and Xerxes
in the Ganj Nameh texts, Rawlinson obtained the phonetic
values of thirteen signs, which we now transliterate (with the

[1] *Journal of the Royal Asiatic Society*, X (1846).

inherent vowels represented by raised letters) d^a, a, r^a, y^a, v^a, u, sh^a, kh^a, v^i, i, t^a, s^a, and p^a. But Rawlinson remembered that, according to Herodotus,[2] Xerxes stated he was the son of Darius, the son of Hystaspes, the son of Arsames, the son of Ariaramnes, the son of Teispes, the son of Cyrus, the son of Cambyses, the son of Teispes, the son of Achaemenes. While there were only three royal names in the Ganj Nameh inscriptions, Rawlinson suspected that in the Behistun inscription there might be more. He was right, for the Old Persian version starts thus: "I am Darius the Great King, King of Kings, . . . King of Countries, son of Hystaspes, grandson of Arsames, an Achaemenian. Darius the King says, My father was Hystaspes, Hystaspes' father was Arsames, Arsames' father was Ariaramnes, Ariaramnes' father was Teispes, Teispes' father was Achaemenes." Accordingly, when Rawlinson found a-r^a-sh^a-a-X where "Arsames" was expected, he knew that X = m (now transliterated m^a). Since a-r^a-i-y^a-a-r^a-m^a-Y corresponded in the genealogy to "Ariaramnes," the final sign was n (now n^a). In Z-kh^a-a-m^a-n^a-i-sh^a-i-y^a, "Achaemenes," the first sign could not represent a (for another sign was already identified as a), so Rawlinson correctly took it to stand for ha. The length and character of the Behistun inscription enabled Rawlinson to go further than others could with the decipherment of Old Persian. Copying the text required athletic prowess and considerable daring; deciphering it required knowledge, intelligence, and perseverance.

In 1839 the Afghan War broke out, and in 1840 Rawlinson was appointed political agent in Kandahar. He organized, trained, and led a unit of Persian cavalry, with which he scored a victory in the battle outside Kandahar on May 29, 1842. His military career ended by the close of that year, and he turned

[2] *History* 7:11.

down other opportunities so that he could return to Baghdad, where he would not be too far from Behistun and other sources of cuneiform texts. Colonel Taylor retired from his post as Political Agent in Turkish Arabia, and Rawlinson succeeded him in 1843 wtih headquarters in Baghdad. With two companions he returned to Behistun early in the summer of 1844 and completed copying the Persian and Elamite versions. The tale of how the job was executed with ropes and ladders, by gaining access to the narrow ledges made by the ancient scribes and sculptors, by shifting positions adroitly to evade death— all this is a hair-raising tale that Rawlinson himself has described.[3]

In 1847 Rawlinson returned to Behistun to copy the Babylonian version, which is even harder to reach. It can be copied from below with the aid of a telescope, but Rawlinson wanted to make a paper squeeze of the text—which was particularly important because that surface was being worn away by erosion from the trickling of rain water. This task was too arduous even for Rawlinson, but he found a "wild Kurdish boy" who by climbing like a human fly, fastening pegs in rocky clefts, and attaching ropes from which he swung from position to position, "by hanging on with his toes and fingers to the slight inequalities on the bare surface of the precipice," and other feats of daring and skill, set up a sort of painter's ladder and, under Rawlinson's direction, made the squeeze of the Babylonian version that was destined to open up the whole field of Assyriology.

The Old Persian inscriptions are of historical and linguistic interest in their own right, but their great importance lies in

[3] His account is republished in Leo Deuel, *The Treasures of Time* (Cleveland: World Publishing Co., 1961), pp. 125-31.

the fact that their translation was the key to the Babylonian version of the trilinguals that clarified the vast epigraphical treasures of Babylonia and Assyria. Although the proper names provided the pronunciation of the signs, it was the knowledge of Avestan Persian and Sanskrit that enabled Rawlinson and other European scholars to work out the vocabulary and grammar in detail and to translate the texts correctly. So close is Old Persian to the language of the Avesta that the etymological method was used with considerable success. Words with exactly the same sound and meaning occur often enough in these two closely related forms of ancient Persian. Later in the nineteenth century, fragments of the Aramaic translation of Darius's Behistun text were discovered at Elephantine, in Upper Egypt.[4] Aramaic is a well-known Semitic language, but those fragments merely confirmed what the decipherers had achieved without benefit of bilingual aids: Old Persian had been completely solved the hard way.

As a sample of Old Persian we may note this prayer excerpted from an inscription of Darius at Persepolis, in cuneiform, transliteration, normalization, and translation:[5]

i	ma	a	ma	/	da	ha	ya	a	u	ma	/
imām					dahyāum						
this					land						

[4] Included in Arthur E. Cowley, *Aramaic Papyri of the Fifth Century* B.C. (London: Oxford University Press, 1923).
[5] For the Old Persian inscriptions see R. G. Kent, *Old Persian: Grammar, Texts, Lexicon* (New Haven: American Oriental Society, 2nd ed., 1953).

a	u	ra	ma	za	da	a	/	pa	a	tu	u

Auramazdā
may Ahuramazda

pātuv
protect

va	/	ha	ca	a	/	ha	i	na	a	ya	a

hacā
from

haināyā
(hostile) army

/	ha	ca	a	/	du	u	sha	i	ya	a

hacā
from

dushiyārā
famine

ra	a	/	ha	ca	a	/	da	ra	u	ga	a

hacā
from

draugā
the lie

"May God protect this country from foe, famine and falsehood."

The second language of the Achaemenian trilinguals is Elamite. Unfortunately, Elamite is not related to any well-known language, and so etymology is of little help. Yet we know the meaning of the Elamite version because it is a translation of the Old Persian in the trilinguals, and one could not ask for a better bilingual key.

Since the Elamite version uses 111 signs, the script was recognized as a syllabary. The absence of word-dividers made the analysis more difficult, but (as Grotefend noted in 1837) male personal names are preceded by a vertical wedge (following the Sumero-Akkadian tradition).

Niels Ludwig Westergaard (1815–1878), who copied texts at Persepolis and Naqsh-e-Rustam in 1843, had the distinction of being the first copyist at those sites who understood what he was copying. He not only worked on proper names in the Elamite version, but he was also the first to transliterate an Elamite passage. Further progress had to await the publication of the Elamite version of the Behistun text by Edwin Norris of London in 1853, which increased the number of names read from forty to ninety. Thereby most of the phonetic values for the Elamite syllabic signs were established. Since the meaning of the text was supplied by the Old Persian text, a grammar and lexicon could be worked out. However, our linguistic comprehension of Elamite is still lagging behind our highly refined knowledge of Old Persian and Babylonian, because Elamite is virtually isolated linguistically. Moreover, Elamite never became important outside of western Iran.

A lot of hard and honest work has gone into Elamite, but its decipherment followed from the real pioneer work on the Old Persian, while the great importance of the trilinguals emanated from the decipherment of the Babylonian version. Realizing this, Rawlinson gave up his work on the Elamite and concentrated on the Babylonian version. The same may be said of the two other outstanding pioneers in Assyriology —the Irishman Edward Hincks (1792–1866) and the Frenchman Jules Oppert (1825–1905). These gifted scholars had already made contributions to the progress of deciphering Old Persian. Hincks, who happened to be an Anglican clergyman, also played a role in the decipherment of Egyptian, in which he recognized the function of determinatives.

Before the decipherment of Babylonian, it was known that the Babylonian version of the Achaemenian trilinguals was related to texts of Mesopotamia, examples of which had become known in Europe during the eighteenth century. Thousands of cuneiform inscriptions, on clay and on stone, were now to be unearthed by a succession of pioneer archeologists. The head of the French vice-consulate at Mosul, Paul-Émile Botta, in 1843 began to excavate at Khorsabad, an Assyrian capital of Sargon of Assyria, who vanquished the northern kingdom of Israel in 722 B.C. Then in 1845 the Englishman Henry Austen Layard began to excavate at the still more important Assyrian capital of Nineveh.[6] These and other excavators filled the museums of Europe, such as the Louvre and the British Museum, with the inscriptions and art of Mesopotamia. Accordingly, it was evident that the third (i.e., Babylonian) section of the Achaemenian inscriptions was by all odds the most significant one, as Rawlinson and others recognized.

Matching the proper names in the Persian and Babylonian versions made it possible to work out the phonetic values of the Babylonian signs, but the process was long and arduous because of the complexities of the Babylonian system of writing. First of all, Babylonian has over 300 signs. The determinatives and ideograms, which are perfectly clear and helpful today, posed innumerable problems for the pioneers who were trying to make sense of them.

Moreover, Babylonian writing is characterized by both polyphony and homophony. A polyphonous sign has more than one phonetic value; thus, the TAR sign can be read (depending on context) *tar*, *kud*, *ḫas*, *sil*, and *gùg*. Just as context tells us to pronounce *s* as *sh* in "sugar" or in "sure" (and if we pronounce it *s* in this word, we would be saying "sewer," which has a very different meaning), the ancient scribes (like

---

[6] For a recent account, see Deuel, *Treasures of Time*, pp. 99–124. Layard's own account, *Nineveh and Its Remains* (New York: George Putnam, 1849), 2 vols., is not only important but has a charm that no discriminating reader should miss.

the modern Assyriologists) knew what value to ascribe to polyphonous signs, depending on context. The script is also characterized by homophony; different signs with the same pronunciation. Thus, there are no fewer than nine entirely different signs with the value of *a*. (Compare *g*, *j*, *s*, and *z* with the sound of *zh* in "rouge," "Jacques," "pleasure," and "azure.")

There are still other peculiarities in Akkadian writing. In addition to signs to be read as *ba, bi, bu, ka, ki, ku*, etc., following the consonant-vowel pattern, and as *ab, ib, ub, ak, ik, uk*, etc., following the vowel-consonant pattern, there are others like *bab, ban, buk, kap, kan, kub*, etc., following the consonant-vowel-consonant pattern. Therefore, a word like *na-ar-ka-ab-tu*, "chariot," can also be spelled *nar-ka-ab-tu, na-ar-kab-tu*, or *nar-kab-tu*. Moreover, the scribes often enjoyed showing off their education by writing the same word in different ways in the same inscription.

In 1850 Rawlinson, after successfully translating a fairly long historic text in Akkadian, admitted that after he had mastered every Babylonian sign and word that could be ascertained on the trilinguals, he was more than once on the verge of abandoning his work when he tried to apply his knowledge to the Assyrian inscriptions. It takes an Assyriologist who knows the material to sympathize with and understand the magnitude of Rawlinson's frustrations, which repeatedly brought him to the verge of despair.

In the 1840's Grotefend identified the names of Darius, Xerxes, Cyrus, and Hystaspes in the Babylonian texts. He also recognized a group of signs on bricks from Babylonia as the name of Nebuchadnezzar, although he could not read the individual signs that comprised it.

In Sweden, Isidor Löwenstern correctly advocated the

Semitic character of Akkadian in 1845. The close relationship of Akkadian to well-known languages such as Hebrew and Arabic made it possible to use the etymological method successfully, provided that it is controlled by the simultaneous use of the contextual method. It was therefore only a matter of time until Akkadian lexicography and grammar were worked out with the high degree of refinement that typifies them today.

Hincks grasped the nature of Babylonian writing when, in 1850, he stated that no sign ever stood for a consonant alone but only for a whole syllable. It was he who recognized that the syllables were of three types (*ba, ab, bab*). Hincks also realized that a sign could be polyphonous, and, for that matter, the same sign could serve as an ideogram, a syllable, or a determinative. He moreover identified a number of determinatives including those that indicate gods, countries, and cities.

The excavator Botta discovered that the same word might be written ideographically or syllabically. He noted that in the inscriptions from Sargon's palace, variants of the same text confronted him with the same word or name written briefly via an ideogram and spelled out at greater length syllabically. To take a simple example: the Akkadian word for "king" is *sharru*, which is usually written with the single KING ideogram, but it could be spelled out *sha-ar-ru* with three signs. Important contributions can be made by amateurs (and Botta was not a professional orientalist or philologian) at an early stage of a subject when everything is yet to be done, and the pioneering spirit can by itself produce useful results. To-day Assyriology is so highly developed that a newcomer, no matter how brilliant, cannot hope to add anything valuable to Assyriology before learning the subject at the modern level. A tyro can hardly identify a new sign, a new word, or a new grammatical form that is not in the published sign lists, dictionaries, or grammars. Real pioneering is not at home in highly developed disciplines.

By the middle of the nineteenth century, pioneers like Rawlinson and Hincks were able to read and translate Akkadian texts. During the three thousand years of cuneiform writing, the script had changed considerably. Moreover, in one and the same period different styles of script were used for different purposes. For instance, the Code of Hammurapi is written in archaic characters on a stone stela, whereas a much simpler form of the signs appears on the clay tablets from Hammurapi's reign. There are also geographical and chronological differences in Sumero-Babylonian writing. A scholar might be perfectly at home in the Akkadian Cuneiform of the Achaemenian period yet unable to recognize the same signs in their earlier and more complicated forms two millennia earlier. Hincks clarified the matter when he identified as duplicates two inscriptions, one in Old Babylonian and the other in Neo-Babylonian characters.

The achievement of the pioneers was far from generally recognized. Scholars accustomed to texts in well-known languages and in familiar alphabets, like Latin and Greek, could not always take in their stride the complexities of Akkadian Cuneiform with its ideograms, polyphony, and homophony. To settle the matter, the Royal Asiatic Society of London took a dramatic step suggested by William Henry Fox Talbot, a mathematician and the inventor of Talbotype photography, who had become deeply immersed in Assyriology. It happened that in 1857 Fox Talbot, Rawlinson, Hincks, and Oppert were all in London. Each was given a copy of a cylinder of Tiglathpileser I that had just been discovered, with instructions to work on it independently and submit their solutions sealed. When their communications were unsealed and opened, it was found that their interpretations were in essential agreement, with the result that the decipherment of Akkadian was not only in fact accomplished but also generally recognized. Even so, not all the denigration and sniping were over. In 1876, A. von Gutschmid attacked the decipherment so virulently that a productive Assyriologist, E. Schrader, felt obliged in 1878 to defend the subject against the attack. What E. Meyer says of Von Gutschmid can be applied to most of the destructive critics who have opposed any of the sound decipherments: "Such distrust concerning the reliability of the foundations of the decipherment would have vanished immediately, if critics like V. Gutschmid had taken the trouble to learn the first elements of the script."[7]

To convey a more concrete notion of how Babylonian was deciphered, we shall examine a few assorted texts to illustrate various aspects of the evidence.

The names and the meaning of the following Babylonian text of Xerxes were supplied by the decipherment of the Old Persian section (cited as "Text 2" on pp. 48–49, above) of the same trilingual (with the phonetic symbols now used by Assyriologists, such as $š$ for "sh" and $ḫ$ for "kh"):

^{m} $ḫi$ — $ši$ —	$ᵓ$ —	ar —	$ši$	KING (= $šarru$)	
Xerxes,				king	

GREAT^u (= $rabû$)	KING (= $šar$)	KING^{pl} (= $šarrâni$)	SON (= $mâr$)
great,	king	of kings,	son

[7] *Geschichte des Altertums* (Stuttgart: J. G. Gotta'sche Buchhandlung, 2nd ed.) II, 2 (1908), pp. 308–9.

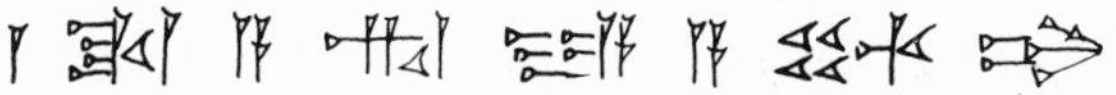

𒈨 𒁕 − 𒀀 − 𒊑 − 𒅀 − 𒀀 − 𒄿 KING (= *šarri*)
^m *da* − *a* − *ri* − *ia* − *a* − *muš* KING (= *šarri*)
of Darius, king

𒈨 𒀀 − 𒄩 − 𒈠 − 𒀭 − �niš − *ši* − ʾ
^m *a* − *ḫa* − *ma* − *an* − *niš* − *ši* − ʾ
Achaemenian

"Xerxes, the great king, the king of kings, son of King Darius, the Achaemenian."

In the transliteration, determinatives and phonetic complements are raised. Thus, ^m precedes male names; ^{pl} indicates plurality; ^ú means that the word it follows ends in -*u*. The ideograms are in capital letters. It is interesting to note that this text gives almost no evidence for the Akkadian language, for outside of the names, the words are written ideographically.

The complexities of the script were felt by the ancient scribes themselves. The scholars of Assyria and Babylonia compiled sign lists, grammatical tables, and other school texts that have been instrumental in reconstructing the ins and outs of the subject.

Because so many tablets were found in the nineteenth century in the Assyrian capitals, particularly at Nineveh, dating to the eighth and seventh centuries B.C., the Assyrian script of that period was adopted as the standard in Assyriological publications. The important library of Assurbanipal (669–631? B.C.) at Nineveh contained such a wealth of texts that the choice of the script of the Sargonid kings of Assyria to serve as the norm was logical. However, about two thousand years of Sumero-Akkadian literature preceded the Sargonids of Assyria. To illustrate the kind of change that took place in a millennium, we shall compare a law of Hammurapi (No. 102

in his Code) as written about 1700 B.C. (on the left) with its
transcription in the Assyrian signs of about 700 B.C.:

šum-ma DAM-GÀR (= *tamkārum*)
If a merchant

a-na ŠAMÁN-LAL (= *šamallîm*)
to a tradesman

KUBABBAR (= *kaspam*) *a-na ta-ad-mi-iq-tim*
silver as a favor

it-ta-di-in-ma
has given,

a-šar   il-   li- ku
where he went

bi- ti- iq-tam
loss

i-   ta-   mar
he has seen,

𒀉 𒀉 𒍑 𒆪 𒌋   𒌇 𒌇 𒍦   𒆬𒌓

qá- qá- ad KUBABBAR (= *kaspim*)
the principal of the silver

𒀀 𒈾 𒁮 𒃼   𒌋𒋫𒅈

a-na DAM-GÀR (= *tamkārim*) *ú-ta-ar*
to the merchant he shall return.

Paraphrasing this law for the sake of clarity, we are to understand, "If a money lender lends money[8] to a trader without interest, and the trader's enterprise runs into a loss, the trader need only return the principal because there are no profits to share."

The interesting thing about this law is the term *qaqqad-*, which means "principal, capital" invested for profit, dividends, or a stipulated rate of interest. Literally, *qaqqad-* means "head"; the spread of the institution of investing capital for dividends or interest from Mesopotamia, via the merchants of Babylonia and Assyria abroad, has left its mark on the capitalist terminology of the West. In West Semitic, Coptic, and Greek, the word for "capital" is derived from a word meaning "head." Latin too reflects the same terminology, for *caput* means not only "head" but also "principal, capital." Indeed, our words for "capital" and "capitalism" are derived from *caput*. The simplest and most basic definition of capitalism is

[8] It is legitimate to use the word "money" in order to convey the sense of the passage. However, coinage was not invented until the seventh century B.C. in Lydia. Hammurapi (*ca.* 1700 B.C.) speaks of "silver" with a value determined by the weight and quality of the metal.

"an economic system which encourages the investment of capital for dividends or interest." The seeds of this system were planted and spread by Sumero-Akkadian businessmen. This is instructive because it illustrates that our culture as a whole reflects its Near East origins; our indebtedness is not limited to a few specialized areas such as religion, the alphabet, and literature. The foundations of our pure sciences and of our economic system are no less rooted in Mesopotamia and the other lands whose antiquities are being opened up by the decipherments.

The reader may have asked himself why the Babylonian scribe who wrote Hammurapi's Code wrote the ideogram KUBABBAR, "silver," when he wanted it to be pronounced *kaspum* "silver," in the excerpt above. It happens that KUBABBAR is the Sumerian word for "silver," and at every turn we see the great impact of Sumerian culture on the Akkadians—in religion, art, writing—to make a long story short, in virtually everything.

In 1850 Hincks discovered that the Babylonian script had been devised for another language, and Oppert gave that language the name we use to designate it: "Sumerian." The Akkadians regarded it as their classical language and therefore taught it in their scribal schools. To do this, they compiled bilingual vocabularies, bilingual grammatical exercises, interlinear translations, etc. For example, there are syllabaries in three columns. The center column lists signs with their Sumerian values on the left and their Akkadian values on the right. One such syllabary includes a section with the numerical ideograms for 10, 20, 30, 40, 50 as follows:[9]

[9] From a syllabary in Friedrich Delitzsch, *Assyrische Lesestücke* (Leipzig: Hinrichs, 1912, 5th ed.), p. 109.

SUMERIAN	SIGN	AKKADIAN
𒌋 *ú*, "ten"	< X	*e-še-ru*, "ten"
ni-iš, "twenty"	<< XX	*eš-ra-a*, "twenty"
e-eš, "thirty"	<<< XXX	*še-la-šá-a*, "thirty"
ni-in, "forty"	<<<< XL	*ir-ba-a*, "forty"
ni-in-nu-u, "fifty"	<<<<< L	*ḫa-áš-šá-a*, "fifty"

The following selection from a comparative Sumero-Akkadian grammatical text illustrates the kind of material that the ancients themselves have left us for reconstructing the inflections of the Sumerian language:[10]

SUMERIAN	AKKADIAN	ENGLISH TRANSLATION
in-lá	*iš-qú-ul*	"he weighed"
in-lá-eš	*iš-qú-lu*	"they weighed"

[10] *Ibid.*, p. 112.

SUMERIAN		AKKADIAN	ENGLISH TRANSLATION
in-lá-e		*i-ša-qal*	"he will weigh"
in-lá-e-ne		*i-ša-qa-lu*	"they will weigh"
in-na-an-lá		*iš-qú-ul-šu*	"he weighed it"
in-na-an-lá-eš		*iš-qú-lu-šu*	"they weighed it"
in-na-an-lá-e		*i-ša-qal-šu*	"he will weigh it"
in-na-an-lá-e-ne		*i-ša-qá-lu-šu*	"they will weigh it"

In spite of the clear evidence for the Sumerian language, its very existence was denied by many scholars. The Assyrians and Babylonians were at least known from the Bible and the classics. But it was too much for some to believe that Assyro-Babylonian civilization was thoroughly indebted to a still older culture whose very name had not survived in any Hebrew, Greek, or Latin document. But how could anyone deny the straightforward evidence? The negators can always find a way. Their leader was Joseph Halévy, who maintained that Sumerian had never existed as a real language but was a kind of ancient cryptographic system invented by the priests and scribes for keeping secrets within their own circle.

Assyriology made a profound impression on Western intellectual life because of its direct bearing on Old Testament history. The invasions of Assyrian and Babylonian kings are recorded in the Bible. Disbelief in the traditional literatures had grown to such proportions that many educated men decided that Old Testament history had been largely invented by Hebrew authors to hoodwink a gullible world. But then came the cuneiform historical documents with the official Mesopotamian version of the very same campaigns described in the Bible. It soon became clear that biblical history is indeed history. Today our ancient history books draw on the evidence of newly deciphered texts, as well as Hebrew and classical sources. We no longer depend on the Bible alone for biblical history concerning Mesopotamian kings named in the Bible, such as Tiglathpileser, Sargon, Sennacherib, Esarhaddon, and Nebuchadnezzar. We possess their own cuneiform annals to confirm, modify, and, above all, to supplement the Hebrew accounts.

This kind of text gave comfort to the conservative members of various religious bodies, but there was another kind of text that was disturbing to them. Scripture, especially in the early chapters of Genesis, contains myths and legends that unsophisticated believers mistook for history. The legend of Noah is a profound document that inculcates the basic attitude necessary for a united mankind. It teaches us that all men, regardless of nation, race, or language, are brothers, descended from one man (Noah) and his wife. It leads up to the remarkable tenth chapter of Genesis, which views the entire known world as a single community of related nations. These are big ideas that mankind must absorb (as attitudes, not as historical or anthropological facts) and apply if our planet is to be worth living in. But believers who naïvely regarded the Deluge as a historical event were shaken upon learning that the same story (albeit devoid of the aspect we have just noted in the Genesis version) circulated among the ancient Mesopotamians long before Genesis was written.

The British excavations at Nineveh unearthed the great library of Assurbanipal (669–631?B.C.), including fragments of the Gilgamesh epic, a twelve-tablet masterpiece unmatched in epic literature until the Homeric epics in Greek. At the British Museum, a self-educated young man named George Smith (1840–1876) took a special interest in the Gilgamesh tablets. He was familiar with the Bible and had a predilection for the early books of the Old Testament. His knack for piecing together broken tablets enabled him to make many valuable joins that helped reconstruct the texts. Smith picked up all he could from his more formally educated associates at the Museum and absorbed what could be learned from books and articles. As a result he developed into a first-class Assyriologist and, because of his special interest in the Gilgamesh tablets, became the outstanding authority on Babylonian myths and legends.

In 1872 Smith observed that the eleventh Gilgamesh tablet narrated a flood story unmistakably connected with the tale of the Deluge in Genesis. Floods are well-nigh universal in legend and myth; but the Genesis and Gilgamesh floods are related, and there is no doubt that the Hebrew depends on the Babylonian rather than vice versa. In both accounts, the flood hero builds the ark and waterproofs it with pitch in accordance with divinely given instructions. Representatives of human, animal, and bird life are taken aboard to perpetuate the various species. The hero determines the availability of dry land after the flood by sending out a series of birds until one does not return, thereby indicating the recession of the waters. The ark lands on a mountain, where the hero gratifies the god(s) with sacrifices. The god(s), smelling the sweet savor, promise(s) never to afflict man with another flood.

Smith's discovery was announced and immediately captured the imagination of secular and religious intellectuals in Europe and America. This was roughly the Age of Darwinism, and the Western world was divided between rationalists eager to tear down Scripture and fundamentalists who wanted to confirm Scripture and repudiate science. Then, as now, there were also the enlightened few who cherished tradition and simultaneously wanted to learn from science and discovery whatever they could to enhance their understanding.

A fragment of the eleventh tablet was missing. Smith estimated its length to be fifteen lines. He wanted to go to Nineveh and dig it up. The *Daily Telegraph* of London subsidized his expedition in exchange for the publication rights. Smith went to Nineveh and in a matter of days found the very fragment (it was seventeen lines long) he had come for! Never has an archeologist dug for something so specific or found it so quickly.[11]

George Smith's discovery of the Babylonian parallel to Noah opened up a whole era of uncovering Mesopotamian parallels to the Old Testament, an era which is far from over. The religious background of Western Europe and America was such that chairs in Assyriology were founded on both sides of the Atlantic. Germany took the lead in refining Assyriology and in training native and foreign students. For a time, American Assyriologists went to Germany for their doctorates, starting with the pioneer American Assyriologist, David Gordon Lyon of Harvard University.[12]

---

[11] See Deuel, *Treasures of Time*, pp. 132–43.
[12] One of the present writer's Assyrian teachers at the University of Pennsylvania was George A. Barton, who had been trained at Harvard by Lyon.

Assyriology flourishes more than Egyptology, in the United States and elsewhere, largely because the importance of Assyriology for biblical studies was stressed and the subject was thereby made relevant for Western culture at a level understood in America and Europe. Egyptology is just as important as Assyriology for biblical studies, but Egyptologists have tended to specialize more narrowly on their own subject, which has therefore remained in relative isolation. In the 1920s, an Egyptian book of wisdom attributed to a sage called Amenemope was discovered and published. Its closeness to a section of the biblical Book of Proverbs is so obvious and detailed that it started a movement that almost brought the Old Testament and Egyptology together. Unfortunately, the chief exponent that emerged, the late A. S. Yahuda, was not the man who could crystallize the union of the two fields. He wrote lucidly and well, knew the Hebrew Bible intimately, and had studied Semitics and Egyptology under the best authorities in Germany, but he was not a critical philologian and his work became discredited—and still remains so—because academicians so often fail to separate the wheat from the chaff.

In important matters, Yahuda was often way ahead of his detractors. He recognized that the correct background for any given part of the Bible must come from the land where that episode is set. The parts dealing with Joseph and Moses are to be understood against Egyptian background, the Book of Esther against Persian background, etc. He rightly understood that the Genesis tales with Mesopotamian background were not (as most scholars then believed) late borrowings from the Exilic period (after 586 B.C.) but from a very early time generally called the Patriarchal Age. What neither he nor his critics realized was that the earliest Hebrews did not have to be in Mesopotamia to absorb their Akkadian background; the latter had permeated the entire Levant, including Palestine, before the Hebrews had conquered the land. Yahuda got no recognition for his labors and insights; instead he reaped a harvest of abuse and ostracism.

While Egyptology tended to remain self-contained, the revelations of Assyriology led to a powerful "Pan-Babylonian" movement throughout the West but especially in Germany. It was sometimes called "Babel and Bible," implying that virtually everything in the Old Testament stemmed from Mesopotamia. Around the turn of the century, even the ordinary man on the street in Germany was concerned with *Babel und Bibel*.[13] It ran its course and eventually became discredited because of its one-sidedness, but actually not even its greatest advocates fully appreciated the magnitude of Mesopotamian influence on the Hebrews as well as on the entire East Mediterranean. It turns out that Babylonian was the international language used throughout the East Mediterranean—in Egypt, Palestine, Lebanon, Syria, Anatolia, and Cyprus. Babylonian inscriptions of the second millennium B.C. have even been found in Greece at Thebes and on Cythera.

The upshot of the matter is that the faith of our fathers and grandfathers was shaken simultaneously by the discoveries of science and archeology. Darwin and his peers came up with evidence that was seen as challenging the accuracy of the Creation in Genesis. George Smith and a whole generation of Assyriologists produced translations of tablets that were regarded as undermining the uniqueness of the Hebrew Deluge and the other early biblical narratives. We and our children

[13] The controversy it provoked is reflected in Friedrich Delitzsch, *Babel and Bible: Two Lectures on the Significance of Assyriological Research for Religion* (Chicago: Open Court Publishing Co., 1903). Delitzsch had to defend himself against invective and vilification that he abhorred "with profound disgust" and described as "mental and moral depravity" (p. 167).

still suffer from the insecurity and confusion that resulted from the twofold assault on tradition.

The simple truth is that Genesis cannot be used as a text-book on geology, any more than *The Origin of Species* can take the place of the Ten Commandments or the Sermon on the Mount. Any enlightened person needs science and tradition, each in its own place and taken on its own terms. There is no more contradiction in this than in the statement that to live we need air as well as food.

The enlightened man must know about the decipherments and the literatures that they have unlocked. Otherwise, one can succumb to various fundamentalisms, such as the view that Homeric epic was an Olympian miracle revealed to a hitherto benighted mankind or that a revelation on Sinai gave the first ray of light to a world engulfed in barbarism. To the contrary, we know that the Bible and Homer are both culminations of highly developed and literate ancient civilizations. We can understand the Bible and the classics only against the background of their foundations as recorded in the cuneiform and Egyptian texts and in the monuments associated with those texts. The value of the decipherments lies not so much in the solving of riddles but in the contents and nature of the texts that they have opened. As a result of archeological discovery and the decipherments, we not only perceive the prehistory of the Bible and the classics, but we also see how they towered above their predecessors and contemporaries.

In Germany, Friedrich Delitzsch (1850–1923) did much to raise the level of Assyriology to new heights and trained a host of disciples. His Assyrian dictionary remained the best until the great Chicago Assyrian Dictionary, which is being published in fascicles. His *Assyrische Lesestücke* was the best reading book for half a century and is still useful. Arthur

Ungnad, who wrote the most lucid Akkadian grammar, was another outstanding Assyriologist; in its revised edition this concise book still provides the best means of learning the structure of the language.[14]

Bruno Meissner published a two-volume work called *Babylonien und Assyrien*,[15] covering the whole range of ancient Mesopotamian civilization. Newer books have appeared that should be used for bringing the subject up to date,[16] but they have not replaced *Babylonien und Assyrien* as the authoritative work. Meissner also prepared on cards the materials for an Akkadian lexicon, which one of the ablest living Assyriologists, Wolfram von Soden, has processed for publication; it, too, is now appearing in fascicles. Less exhaustive than the huge Chicago Assyrian Dictionary, which is the product of complex teamwork, the Meissner-Soden lexicon is of more manageable proportions and has inner consistency because it was compiled by a single authority and carefully revised by another, neither of whom was subject to outside pressures for alterations or compromise. Von Soden is also the author of the detailed grammar of the Akkadian dialects, which is indispensable for the advanced student.[17]

In spite of the abundant Sumerian materials—including bilinguals and school texts—Sumerian linguistics lags behind

[14] Arthur Ungnad's Akkadian grammar has been revised by Lubor Matouš and published under the title of *Grammatik des Akkadischen* (Munich: Beck, 1964).

[15] B. Meissner, *Babylonien und Assyrien* (Heidelberg: C. Winter, 1920–25), 2 vols.

[16] E.g., H. W. F. Saggs, *The Greatness That Was Babylon* (New York: Hawthorn Books, 1962); and A. Leo Oppenheim, *Ancient Mesopotamia: Portrait of a Dead Civilization* (Chicago: University of Chicago Press, 1964).

[17] W. von Soden, *Grundriss der akkadischen Grammatik* (Rome: Pontifical Biblical Institute, 1952).

Akkadian because Akkadian is Semitic, whereas Sumerian has no close relationship to any other known language. A Frenchman, François Thureau-Dangin, rendered an outstanding service in translating royal Sumerian unilinguals in 1907 so accurately that he provided a basis for all future work.[18] His German counterpart, Arno Poebel, was often in polemic conflict with him on details. Poebel's Sumerian grammar, published in 1923,[19] was a great step forward in systematizing the rules of the Sumerian language. On the other hand, the transliteration he employs is often incomprehensible to the present generation of cuneiformists. Thureau-Dangin's system of transliterating Sumero-Akkadian has prevailed. Poebel migrated to America and ended his career at the Oriental Institute of the University of Chicago. It was there that he trained two of the foremost living Sumerologists, Samuel Noah Kramer and Thorkild Jakobsen.

The best available grammar of Sumerian is limited to the texts of one ruler, Gudea of the city-state of Lagash, *ca.* 2000 B.C., whose inscriptions constitute the most classical expression of Sumerian. Adam Falkenstein (1906–1966) of Germany produced a comprehensive study of Gudea's texts with a detailed grammar of them, covering the phonology, morphology, and syntax.[20] While the general meaning of the texts is clear, numerous passages are still interpreted differently by the top Sumerologists, nor is there always unanimity on grammatical analysis. Sumerian is the world's first great classical language;

---

[18] F. Thureau-Dangin, *Die sumerischen und akkadischen Königsinschriften* (Leipzig: Hinrichs, 1907).

[19] A. Poebel, *Grundzüge der sumerischen Grammatik* (Rostock: privately printed by the author, 1923).

[20] A. Falkenstein, *Grammatik der Sprache Gudeas von Lagaš* (Rome: Pontifical Biblical Institute, 1950), 2 vols.

its impact through Akkadian has been enormous and still reverberates in our culture.

The Akkadian scribes, trained as they were in bilingualism from the very start because of their Sumerian heritage, were (unlike the Egyptians) generally ready to use their script for other languages and to compile bilingual, trilingual, and even quadrilingual texts for didactic purposes. An important people in the Akkadian sphere during the entire second millennium were the Hurrians. For a while there was a Hurrian kingdom, called Mitanni, in northwest Mesopotamia. During the early part of the Amarna Age (late fifteenth and early fourteenth centuries B.C.), when the Pharaohs corresponded in Babylonian with other rulers all over the civilized world, the Mitannian king Tushratta wrote a very long letter in Hurrian, as well as other letters in Babylonian, to Amenophis III. Tushratta was a quite repetitious correspondent, so that even though his Hurrian letter is not a bilingual, we know from his Akkadian letters the things he had on his mind. Besides, the script of the Hurrian letter is identical with the script of the Akkadian correspondence and is therefore pronounceable. The ideograms and determinatives provide welcome clues as to the meaning of many words.

The slow and imperfect decipherment of Hurrian is due to the exotic affinities of the language, which is unrelated to Semitic, Indo-European, Sumerian, and practically everything else. Meanwhile, bilingual inscriptions in Akkadian and Hurrian have turned up and also school texts that list Hurrian words parallel to their equivalents in Sumerian, Akkadian, or Ugaritic (two tablets listing words in all four languages in parallel columns have been found at Ugarit). Hurrian texts written in the Ugaritic alphabet have also been found. And yet the Hurrian letter of Tushratta remains the chief source of our knowledge of the language. By working with phrases containing known personal names and by matching up Hurrian and Akkadian phrases in the Amarna letters, Hurrian vocabulary, grammar, and syntax have made some definitive progress. For instance, *ᵐni-im-mu-u-ri-a-aš* LAND *mis-sí-ir-ri-e-we-ni-eš iw-ri-iš* means "Nimmuria (one of the known names of Amenophis III), King (*iwriš*) of Egypt" and *ᵐar-ta-ta-a-maš am-ma-ti-iw-wu-uš* means "Artatama, my grandfather" (known as such from Tushratta's Akkadian letters). The following are among the expressions in Akkadian and Hurrian that can also be paired: Akkadian GOD^{pl} *li-me-eš-še-ru-uš*, "may the gods allow it" = Hurrian GOD^{pl} *e-e-en-na-šu-uš na-ak-ki-te-en;* and Akkadian *ki-i-me-e a-mi-lu-ú-tum* GOD*Šamaš i-ra-'-am-šu*, "as mankind loves the Sun" = Hurrian *i-nu-ú-me-e-ni-i-in* GOD*Ši-mi-gi tar-šu-an-niš . . . ta-a-ti-a*. In the latter pair, Hurrian *inu* = Akkadian *kīmē*, "as"; Hurrian *Shimigi* = Akkadian *Shamash*, "Sun (god)"; Hurrian *taršu-anni-* = Akkadian *amēlūtum*, "mankind"; Hurrian *tat-* = Akkadian *ra'āmu*, "to love".[21]

Toward the end of the nineteenth century, scholars such as Peter Jensen and Daniel G. L. Messerschmidt laid the foundations for interpreting Hurrian texts by matching such Akkadian and Hurrian equivalent phrases and then proceeding from the known Akkadian to the unknown Hurrian. Bit by bit many lexical and grammatical details have been squeezed out of numerous texts, but the specialized nature of the latter and the lack of relationship with a well-known linguistic

[21] See Johannes Friedrich, *Extinct Languages* (New York: Philosophical Library, 1957), pp. 79–81. (The second edition of the original German book *Entzifferung verschollener Schriften und Sprachen* [Heidelberg: Springer-Verlag], appeared in 1966.) The latest comprehensive treatment of Hurrian is Frederick William Bush, *A Grammar of the Hurrian Language* (Ann Arbor, Mich.: University Microfilms, 1965).

family leave us with an inadequate knowledge of the language. We have, for example, grammars of Hurrian that give learned discussions of grammatical features, but when a new Hurrian text is found, it is only with the greatest difficulty that the best-qualified scholars can eke out the meaning of even a fraction thereof.

Armenia nurtured an ancient civilization. Its iron and copper mines were important in a world that needed metals for its technology and daily life. The biblical flood story has Noah's Ark landing on the Mountains of Ararat[22] (= Urartu, as Armenia is called in the cuneiform records). This can only mean that Armenia was considered an important center when the Genesis Deluge account was formulated. Located in the mountains where Turkey, the Soviet Union, Iran, and Iraq now meet or come near each other, Armenia was in a position to resist the onslaught of the Assyrian armies more successfully than many of the other targets of Assyrian imperialism. Indeed, from the ninth through the seventh century B.C., Urartu was the most effective rival of Assyria, and until 714 B.C., when Sargon of Assyria invaded and weakened Urartu, the Urarteans were the rivals of the Assyrians in claiming to be the world's leading power.

Around 1000 B.C. the Hurrians disappeared from the scene at large except in Urartu, where they held on down to the general upheaval associated with the Scythian invasion around 600 B.C. Urartean is fairly closely related to Hurrian. There are about 200 Urartean inscriptions from Turkey, Iran, and the Soviet Union, including two Akkadian-Urartean bilingual stelas. Additional clues to the meaning come from the ideograms and determinatives that are found in the Sumero-Akkadian system used for writing Urartean. The limited

[22] Genesis 8:4.

scope and character of the texts, combined with the fact that the language is related only to the imperfectly known Hurrian, leave us with an all-too-sketchy lexical and grammatical picture of Urartean.[23] Work on the subject is fully justified, no matter how lean the pickings may be. Urartu, after all, was one of the two leading nations in the Near East for over a century. Too little is known about it. Whatever we can learn about the Urarteans and their language is likely to be more important than the casual observer might expect.

Outside of Sumerian and Akkadian themselves, the most important language written in their script is Hittite, which is discussed in the next chapter.

---

[23] Friedrich, who has done detailed work on Urartean, gives a succinct account of its partial decipherment in *Extinct Languages*, pp. 81–82.

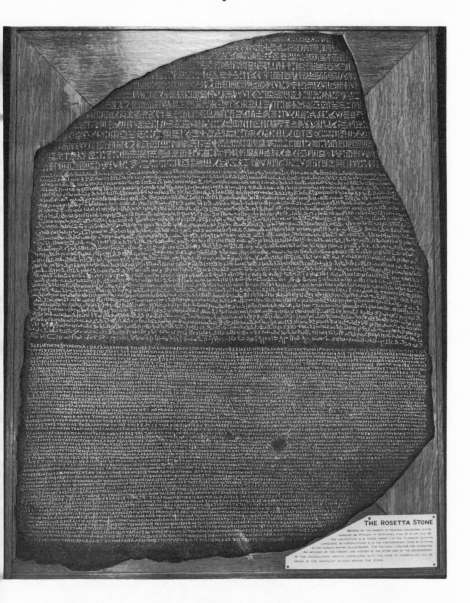

THE ROSETTA STONE. This triple account of the Decree of Memphis was the main key for deciphering Egyptian. The bottom third, being Greek, was the clue to the two Egyptian versions in hieroglyphic (top) and Demotic (middle) writing. *(Courtesy the British Museum.)*

A LIMESTONE FUNERARY STELA of Senresew made for him by his wife Hormes, who is shown with him before a small table of offerings. The hieroglyphic text represents the conventional offering formula. (XVIII Dynasty, Egyptian.) *(Courtesy the Brooklyn Museum.)*

A SCRIBE'S WOODEN EXERCISE BOARD. The Hieratic script spells out a portion of the "Instruction of Amenemmes I." (XVIII Dynasty, Egyptian.) *(Courtesy the Brooklyn Museum.)*

IV

THE LOWER HALF OF A LIMESTONE STELA of the steward of Hathor-
Neferhotep, from the Temple of Hu, illustrating Demotic writing.
(Egyptian, not earlier than XXI Dynasty.) *(Courtesy the Brooklyn
Museum.)*

HAMMURAPI'S CODE. The seated figure is Shamash, the Sun god who is concerned with justice. King Hammurapi, who promulgated the divinely sanctioned law, reverently stands before the deity. The code is inscribed on the rest of the stela's surface. *(Courtesy the Louvre.)*

THE TRILINGUAL AUTOBIOGRAPHY OF DARIUS AT BEHISTUN. "I am Darius the Great King, King of Kings, . . . King of countries" At risk of life and limb, Rawlinson spent years copying the text of the Behistun trilingual. At the left are two officers of the Great King. Then comes Darius himself in heroic scale, facing the rebellious leaders whom he had to quell in order to reconstitute the Empire. The hands of the captured rebels are tied behind them. Above the figures is the bust of the god Ahuramazda set in a winged solar disc. (*Courtesy George G. Cameron.*)

A DETAIL (the head of Darius) from the Behistun trilingual, shown on the facing page.

A WINGED DEITY pollinating stylized trees, symbolizing fertility. This is an alabaster relief from the Northwest Palace of King Assur-nasir-pal II at Nimrud. (Assyrian, 880 B.C.) *(Courtesy the Brooklyn Museum.)*

THE HAND of the figure shown on the facing page, with cuneiform inscription.

THE PHAISTOS DISC, whose pictographs were stamped on the clay while it was still wet and soft, is a forerunner of printing. The Disc is the most striking inscription bequeathed by Minoan civilization. (*Courtesy the Heraklion Museum.*)

5

CUNEIFORM AND HIEROGLYPHIC HITTITE

The history, language, and literature of the Hittites are of exceptional interest. Hittite is the oldest recorded Indo-European language; it is related to Sanskrit, Greek, Latin, English, and most of the other well-known languages of Europe. In the second millennium B.C., the Hittites were a major force on the international scene and in the fourteenth and thirteenth centuries rivaled, and sometimes eclipsed, Egypt and the Mesopotamian powers as the

world's leading nation. Early in the twelfth century, when
the whole East Mediterranean was in a state of turmoil, the
Hittite capital of Hattusas (now near Boğazköy in central
Turkey)was destroyed by invaders and never rebuilt.

In retrospect, it is surprising that this great empire, which
was very much in the mainstream of world history, had been
for all intents and purposes lost to human memory. There
are references to the Hittites in Scripture,[1] but it was the
decipherment of Egyptian and cuneiform that provided so
much information on the Hittites that Orientalists realized
how important the Hittites were. In a temple at Karnak there
is inscribed a text dealing with the treaty (*ca.* 1280 B.C.)
between Ramses II and the Hittite king Hattusilis III. Many
Assyrian texts refer to Hattu ("Hittite land"), as the West is
sometimes called, including Syria and Palestine. The tablets
found in Egypt at Tell el-Amarna since 1887 include letters
exchanged between the Egyptian and Hittite kings. Gradually
it was realized that the Hittites had not only been a major
Near Eastern power but had also dominated the land bridge
joining the cuneiform and Semitic spheres to the Greeks in
Ionia.

The rediscovery of the Hittites was based on scattered bits
of curious evidence that did not fit into the conventional
scheme of things.[2] By 1870 Egyptian hieroglyphs and Mesopotamian Cuneiform had left the impression that, before
Hebrew and Greek history, the Near East had only two
main elements: Egyptian and Assyro-Babylonian. But very

---

[1] Genesis 10:15; 23:3, 5, 7, 10; Exodus 3:8, 17; Deuteronomy 7:1; 20:17;
Joshua 3:10; Judges 3:5; Ezekiel 16:3, 45; etc.
[2] The routine scholar tends to be concerned with "normal" phenomena in
keeping with accepted opinion. The pioneer is attracted to atypical data,
whose investigation may lead to new horizons.

modest indications of a third culture had come to light. In 1812 the Anglo-Swiss explorer Johann Ludwig Burckhardt (1784–1817) noticed a stone in Hamath, North Syria, bearing pictographs quite unlike Egyptian hieroglyphs. No one paid much attention to this until two American diplomats found it and four similarly inscribed stones in Hamath in 1870 and published their findings in 1872.[3]

The man who first associated the Hamath hieroglyphs with the Hittites was the Reverend Archibald Henry Sayce (1846–1933), Professor of Comparative Philology and Assyriology at Oxford University. Exemplifying nineteenth-century scholarship, he was grounded in classics and Hebrew. The spirit of intellectual adventure had led him to the expanding frontiers of history and to the languages and literatures that were emerging during the century of the great decipherments.

In due time, texts with the same hieroglyphs as those found at Hamath turned up elsewhere. With the exception of lead scrolls inscribed in a cursive form of the same script, found at Assur, the evidence is limited to seals and to stone inscriptions from Anatolia, North Syria (and now also Thebes in Greece). Sayce reasoned that those two contiguous areas (i.e., Anatolia and North Syria) had once been ruled by the Hittite kings. Specifically, the hieroglyphs inscribed on stone were found at Yazilikaya (near Boğazköy), at the pass of Karabel (near Smyrna), at Ivriz (in the Taurus Mountains), and at the North Syrian sites of Hamath, Aleppo, and Carchemish. The most impressive are in the out-of-door mountain shrine of Yazilikaya, which seemed to be the na-

---

[3] See the accounts by Ernst Doblhofer, *Voices in Stone* (New York: Viking Press, 1961), pp. 150–53; P. E. Cleator, *Lost Languages* (New York: John Day, 1959), pp. 115–16; and especially William Wright (1837–1899), in C. W. Ceram, *Hands on the Past* (New York: Alfred A. Knopf, 1966), pp. 270–76.

tional shrine, near what accordingly appeared to be the national capital buried under a great mound not far from the village of Boğazköy. Thus, in a few vestiges of the undeciphered Hittite monuments, Sayce perceived the presence and extent of the Hittite Empire. His views were, of course, hotly contested. Most scholars like to have a great preponderance of evidence (and even then there are many who will not face the facts). Outstanding innovators like Sayce work differently; they sense the significance of odd bits of material and generalize from them. If the theory is correct—and the reconstruction is as important as they claim—further evidence will be found. Sayce had the satisfaction of discovering the Hittite Empire and of having his pioneering views corroborated, beyond his hopes and dreams, in his lifetime.

The Amarna tablets found in 1887 and thereafter began to fill the gaps in our knowledge, for they include references to the Hittites and a letter written by the great Hittite king Shuppiluliuma to the Pharaoh. But the Amarna tablets also include two letters in Hittite from Arzawa in Asia Minor.[4] The script is the Akkadian of the Amarna Age and can be pronounced. The ideograms and names are clues to the meaning. The Norwegian Assyriologist J. A. Knudtzon came out in 1902 with a publication on the Arzawa letters in which he correctly concluded that the language was Indo-European. He noted, for example, that *e-es-tu*, which from context has to mean "may it be," is the Indo-European *esto* "may it be." This important discovery was right, and if Knudtzon had had the courage of his convictions, he would have been the

---

[4] The best edition is still J. A. Knudtzon, *Die El-Amarna-Tafeln* (Leipzig: Vorderasiatische Bibliothek, 1907–15). A more recent edition is S. A. B. Mercer, *The Tell el-Amarna Tablets* (Toronto: Macmillan, 1939), 2 vols. In both editions the Arzawa tablets are texts Nos. 31 and 32.

decipherer of Hittite. When his views promptly evoked sharp criticism, however, he retracted his discovery and missed his chance to be the great decipherer for which he was qualified by knowledge and intelligence, but not by disposition.

A discoverer must not allow himself to be shouted down by the critics who are ever present to discredit any major contribution. However stubborn Grotefend may have been (and he was on occasion more stubborn than necessary or desirable), he earned his laurels not only by cracking the Old Persian system but also by retaining his faith in his work. Champollion and Rawlinson ran into their full share of opposition, but they never retracted their decipherments or abandoned their labors. Knudtzon's sterling reputation as an Assyriologist endures, but as a decipherer he was weighed in the scales and found wanting. His lack of self-confidence wiped out his discovery, so that it had to be rediscovered years later by a real pioneer. It is only fair to say, however, that the latter had at his disposal a mass of evidence that was still under the ground in 1902.

Meanwhile, fragments of tablets in the same language as the Arzawa letters had been found near Boğazköy by a French explorer, E. Chantre, in 1893. Accordingly, it was clear that whatever the linguistic affinities of the Arzawa letters, they were in the same language of the Hittites used also at Boğazköy, which presumably marked the capital of the Hittite Empire. Sayce realized this and tried to get the British to start excavating there. But Germany had become the main center of cuneiform studies, and the Kaiser was interested in the project. Moreover, the German ambassador in Constantinople was influential. So the Germans got the permit to excavate, and they sent the Assyriologist Hugo Winckler to head the expedition in 1905.

After preliminary work in that year, Winckler conducted a major operation at Boğazköy in 1906-8. He uncovered the royal archives, finding more than 10,000 tablets, among them the Akkadian version of the treaty between Hattusilis III and Ramses II, long known from the Egyptian version inscribed at Karnak.[5] The style, script, names, and contents of the Boğazköy archives left no doubt as to their historical period. Belonging to the Amarna Age and the Rameside Age that followed it, the Hittite archives came from the fourteenth and thirteenth centuries B.C. They included a great number of tablets in the native Hittite language. In addition to standard Hittite, some of the tablets contained passages in cognate dialects called "Luwian" and "Palaic." Something is known about Luwian, thanks largely to tablets with alternating Hittite and Luwian sections dealing with the same ritual topics.

Moreover, an unrelated language known as "Hattic" was represented; it was the speech of pre-Hittite inhabitants who had left a deep impression on Hittite religion so that certain rituals were accompanied by Hattic recitations. Hittite-Hattic bilingual rituals have provided us with some knowledge of Hattic. Akkadian, as the international language, was used extensively. Sumerian, as the classical language of the cuneiform world, had its place too. Hurrian was also important there. School texts from Hattusas sometimes added Hittite to the Sumerian and Akkadian columns, which eventually helped to teach us some of the details of the Hittite language.

But the main clue to interpreting the Hittite texts was the abundance of ideograms (both Sumerograms and Akkadograms) in the unilinguals. Often the Hittite scribes express

[5] Note Leo Deuel, *The Treasures of Time* (Cleveland: World Publishing Co., 1961), pp. 256–67, for Winckler's own story.

the root of a verb or noun ideographically and add the grammatical endings as phonetic complements. This gives us the Hittite inflexions, even as the ideograms are a clue to the meaning of the passage. There are also bilinguals and even translations of known literary as well as historic texts. For example, fragments of the Gilgamesh Epic in Hittite (and Hurrian) translation have been found at Boğazköy. There is accordingly no dearth of material for elucidating the Hittite language. But we must not get the idea that the task was easy for the pioneers; like all pioneering work, the first great strides in Hittitology look easy only in retrospect.

A young Assyriologist from Prague had been exposed to the fine school of linguistic science that had grown in his native city. Those were the days before the dissolution of the Austro-Hungarian Empire, and the young scholar Bedřich Hrozný (1879–1952) happened to be teaching in Vienna as World War I was breaking out. Endowed with the necessary combination of curiosity, originality, brilliance, and daring and equipped with a sound knowledge of cuneiform and linguistics, he embarked on a project to prepare copies of Hittite tablets from Boğazköy for publication. Happily the task provided him with the opportunity of investigating the character and affinities of the Hittite language.

At first some hope was attached to fragments of trilingual dictionaries, in which Sumerian words were rendered in Akkadian and in Hittite in three parallel columns. But such lists contain mostly rare words that are of little use in reading normal texts, and they provide little or none of the grammatical elements. Hrozný therefore worked mainly with unilingual Hittite texts, where the ideograms (both Sumerograms and Akkadograms) provided clues as to the meaning, so that he could make further inferences from context concerning

the words and suffixes in true Hittite. The following is one
of the key passages interpreted by Hrozný:

nu BREAD-*an e-iz-za-at-te-ni*
wa-a-tar-ma e-ku-ut-te-ni

Hrozný saw that the passage consisted of two parallel
halves, which balanced each other, as is clear from the rhyming
endings of each half. BREAD is a Sumerogram, whose meaning
was already known. Parallel to "bread" is *wa-a-tar*, an Indo-
European word cognate with English "water"! Since one
eats bread and drinks water, Hrozný was able to infer the
meanings of the two verbs. The first is cognate with German
essen, Latin *edere*, and English *eat*. The suffix -*n* in BREAD-*an*
is the accusative case ending (related to -*n* in Greek). A
number of other passages showed that *nu* and enclitic -*ma*
mean something like "now . . . then . . ." or "both . . . and
. . ." The whole passage is to be translated: "Now bread you
eat; water then you drink."

This kind of evidence left no doubt in Hrozný's mind:
Hittite was Indo-European. With grammatical inflexions and
basic vocabulary pointing in the same direction, a real pioneer
like Hrozný did not waver. Before he was through, he had
set Hittite on its true course, so that today Cuneiform Hittite
is one of the best-known languages recovered in the Age of
the Decipherments. Moreover, it has exerted a great influence
on Indo-European linguistics, for Hittite is the first recorded
Indo-European language and is full of interesting phenomena
and new evidence.

Hrozný made a detailed study of tablets containing a Hittite law code. The phraseology in such codes was familiar
from other cuneiform texts such as Hammurapi's Code, in

which the common formula is: "If a person commits such and such an offense, he is to be punished in such and such a way." Accordingly, Hrozný knew the general meaning of sections like the following, from the Sumerograms and Akkadograms and could attribute the correct sense and grammatical analysis to the Hittite words: *ták-ku* LÚ-ULÙ^{LU} EL-LUM QA-AS-SÚ *na-aš-ma* GÌR-ŠU *ku-iš-ki tu-wa-ar-ni-iz-zi nu-uš-še* 20 GÍN KUBABBAR *pa-a-i*. The ideograms (which are in Sumerian or Akkadian or a combination of both) were known to have these meanings: LÚ-ULÙ^{LU}, "man"; EL-LUM, "free"; QA-AS-SÚ, "his hand"; GÌR-ŠU, "his foot"; GÍN, "shekel"; and KUBABBAR, "silver." The sense of the entire law is: "If anybody breaks the hand or foot of a free man, he shall pay 20 shekels of silver to him." Note that *ku-iš-ki*, "anybody," is cognate with Latin *quisque*. *Ták-ku* means "if"; *na-aš-ma*, "or"; *tu-wa-ar-ni-iz-zi*, "breaks"; *nu-uš-še*, "to him"; and *pa-a-i*, "he gives, pays."

On the basis of context, Sumero-Akkadian script and literature, and Indo-European linguistics, Hrozný and his followers have worked out Cuneiform Hittite so that we have good grammars, dictionaries, and all the didactic and reference materials that scholars need for mastering the language and interpreting new texts.[6] It should be noted that Hrozný and other cuneiformists were not in a position to integrate Hittite and the other Indo-European languages with linguistic finesse.

---

[6] Johannes Friedrich has supplied the best introductory tools for the study of Cuneiform Hittite: *Hethitisches Elementarbuch* (Heidelberg: Carl Winter, 1940–46), 2 vols.; *Hethitisches Wörterbuch* (Heidelberg: Carl Winter, 1952, followed by three supplements in 1957, 1961, 1966); and *Hethitisches Keilschrift-Lesebuch* (Heidelberg: Carl Winter, 1960). The standard edition of the Hittite Code is also by him: *Die hethitischen Gesetze* (Leiden: Brill, 1959).

Professional Indo-Europeanists starting with Ferdinand Sommer rendered this service. And even today, Hittitologists come in two groups—the cuneiformists, who take the lead in interpreting the texts, and Indo-Europeanists, who deal with linguistic details and bring the evidence of Hittite to bear on comparative Indo-European.

Unlike Cuneiform Hittite, which is in a known script, Hieroglyphic Hittite had to be deciphered from scratch. We now know that the hieroglyphs express a dialect more closely related to Luwian than to the standard Cuneiform Hittite of Hattusas. Royal seals of the Hittite Empire (*ca.* 1400–1200 B.C.) are written in the hieroglyphs, sometimes accompanied by a cuneiform version. Such bilinguals provided opening wedges in the decipherment.

After the collapse of the Empire early in the twelfth century B.C., Cuneiform Hittite went out of use. However, city-states on the fringe of the Empire in Syria and Cilicia continued to write Hieroglyphic Hittite, and most of the texts come from those areas and date from the tenth to the end of the eighth centuries B.C., when the spread of Assyrian power put an end to the Hittite tradition in those city-states.

As we have already noted, it was in the early 1870s that Sayce identified the hieroglyphs as Hittite. An unappreciated opening wedge for the decipherment, however, had come to light in 1863, when A. D. Mordtmann published a description of a silver boss (subsequently known to be a regular type of royal Hittite seal) with hieroglyphs and cuneiform writing. The seal, which belonged to a dealer, had previously been offered for sale to the British Museum, where Samuel Birch considered it a copy and Henry Rawlinson pronounced it a complete fake. Although the Museum did not buy the seal, it made some wax impressions, from which apparently a number

of copies have been made.[7] In 1880 Sayce made a careful study of it and rightly concluded that it was a bilingual. For a long time it was known as the Tarkondemos Seal; now it is read:

Tarku-muwa KING *me+r(a)-a* LAND
"Tarkummuwa, King of the Land of Mera"

Sayce correctly identified the ideograms for KING and LAND. From other texts, Sayce isolated the ideograms for CITY ( ) and GOD ( ), as well as the nominative ending (*s*) and the accusative ending (*n*). He did not discover their phonetic values;[8] if he had, he might have realized that the language was Indo-European (compare Greek *anthrōpo-s,* "man," in the nominative with *anthrōpo-n* in the accusative). Sayce also noted that the ideogram for GOD preceded all divine names and that therefore it served as a determinative.

Around 1890 the French lawyer and Assyriologist Joachim Ménant (1820–1899) correctly identified the function of the man pointing to himself ( ) as the pronoun first person singular, even as the Egyptian man pointing to himself ( ) designates the same pronoun. This was important because it clarified the style of the Hittite inscriptions that begin "I am so-and-so. . . ."

It was not until the 1930s that four scholars (P. Meriggi,

[7] See No. 69 (p. 24 and Pl. VIII) in C. H. Gordon, "Western Asiatic Seals in the Walters Art Gallery," *Iraq,* VI (1939), 3–34 and Pls. II–XV.
[8] I.e., that the two endings were pronounced *s* and *n,* respectively.

I. Gelb, E. Forrer, and H. Bossert) by their cumulative efforts made further progress with the decipherment. Meriggi got the ideogram for "son," which was of use in interpreting the genealogies. Gelb spotted the word "to make" and correctly transliterated it as *aia*; this word helped establish the close affinity of Hieroglyphic Hittite and Luwian. Forrer recognized a formula of imprecation which was of value in delineating sentence structure. Bossert (1889–1962) read the royal name Warpalawa and the name of the goddess Kupapa. The achievement of the 1930s was largely through the establishment of the phonetic values of signs without the aid of bilinguals. This was done by observing that a particular city or land name (whose category was fixed by the CITY or LAND determinative) occurred only in the inscriptions from one particular place. At Carchemish it was assumed that

was to be read

Kar — ka — me CITY

Sometimes this method was controllable by interlocking syllabic repetitions. For instance, Mar'ash (= *Gur-gu-ma* in Cuneiform Hittite) and Hamath (= *Ha-ma-tu* in Cuneiform) both have the syllable *ma*. At Gurgumma and Hamath, respectively, the following names could therefore be read thus:

Ku+r(a) — ku — ma   CITY

and

A — ma — tu   LAND

At Tuwanuwa (Tyana), the following name could be read

with confidence, thanks to the repetition of the syllable *wa* (which is the kind of corroboration found in the repetition of *ku/gu* in Gurgumma). Also, the *tu* ties in with the same sign in *A-ma-tu*, "Hamath":

Tu — wa — n(u) — wa CITY

The Assyrian kings mention in their Annals the names of several Hittite kings such as Muwatali of Gurgumma, Urḫilinu of Hamath, and Warpalawa of Tuwanuwa. Accordingly, if inscriptions from such towns or states can be dated to the periods when those kings ruled, it is possible for their personal names to appear in the inscriptions. With this possibility in mind, the search produced the following royal names:

Mu — wa — ta — li

U+r(a) — ḫi — li — n(a)

Wa+r(a) — pa — la — wa

Between 1933 and 1937 more royal seals were found at Boğazköy, so that scholars learned the hieroglyphic form of the names of most of the Great Kings. Although most of their names are written ideographically, *Mu-ta-li* (= *Mu-wa-ta-li*) is spelled out syllabically, and the queens' names Puduḫepa and Tanuḫepa are also spelled out and automatically provided the reading of the chief goddess of the Hittite mountain shrine of Yazilikaya:

GOD *Ḫa — ba — tu* = cuneiform GOD *Ḫe-bat,* "the goddess Ḫebat." (The third sign can be read *ba* or *pa.*)

After the system of the Hittite hieroglyphs had been cracked the hard way by Meriggi, Gelb, Forrer, and Bossert, a great Phoenician and Hieroglyphic Hittite bilingual at Karatepe in Cilicia came to Bossert's attention after World War II. A king named Azitawadd had ruled there toward the close of the eighth century B.C. and built a palace embellished with reliefs and inscriptions telling about his accomplishments. The Phoenician text (which is by far the longest known Phoenician inscription) is quite intelligible. Bossert, who happened to be stationed permanently in Turkey, fell heir to the Karatepe finds and, of course, understood the importance of the discovery for the elucidation of Hieroglyphic Hittite.[9] Not being a Semitist, Bossert realized that the best way to proceed was to send copies of the Phoenician text to experts in Northwest Semitic and urge them to publish their translations as promptly as possible. Several, including the present writer, did so and within a short time the Phoenician key to the Hieroglyphic version was available. Unfortunately, Bossert did not publish the whole Hieroglyphic version; in fact, he released only sections rearranged to match the phraseology of the Phoenician version. And since the Hittite word order is different from the Phoenician, Bossert transposed the Hittite to agree with the Phoenician sequence, so that we do not always know the order of the Hittite words on the original

[9] Bossert's own account is reproduced by Ceram, *Hands on the Past,* pp. 288–94. For the grammar of Hieroglyphic Hittite and its corpus of texts, see Piero Meriggi, *Manuale di Eteo Geroglifico* (Rome: Edizioni dell'-Ateneo), I (*Grammatica,* 1966), II (*Testi,* 1967).

stone. Bossert has meanwhile died, and the full Hittite version of this important text is still not published. But Bossert's articles leave no doubt that the Karatepe bilingual will greatly advance our knowledge of Hieroglyphic Hittite, particularly in enlarging the vocabulary.

The value of the Karatepe bilingual is enormous, but the first decisive steps in deciphering Hieroglyphic Hittite were made without it. Karatepe confirmed the soundness of the painstaking work done in the 1930s.

The following translation of the Phoenician version will convey an idea of the vocabulary, style, and scope of the Karatepe text:

> I am Azitawadd, the blessed of Baal, the servant of Baal, whom Awarku, King of the Danunites, exalted. Baal made me as a father and a mother to the Danunites. I quickened the Danunites, enlarged the Land of the Plain of Adana, from the rising of the sun to its setting, and in my days the Danunites had every good and plenty and goodness. And I filled the arsenals of Paghar and I multiplied horse upon horse and shield upon shield and camp upon camp by the grace of Baal and the gods. I shattered the insolent (?). And I wiped out all the evil that was in the land. And I erected the house of my lordship in goodness and I did good for the progeny of my lord. And I sat on the throne of his father and made peace with every king. And even (as) in fatherhood (i.e., like a father) every king treated me because of my righteousness, wisdom, and goodness of heart. And I built mighty walls in all the outposts on the borders, in places where there had been bad men with gangs, none of whom had been subservient to the House of Mopsh; but I, Azitawadd, put them under my feet and I built settlements in those places for the Danunites to inhabit in the ease of their hearts. And I subjugated mighty lands in the west, which none of the kings before me had subjugated, but I, Azitawadd, subjugated them, bringing them down and settling them in the extremity of my borders in the east, and Danunites I settled there. And there were in my days, in all the borders of the Plain of Adana, from the rising of

the sun to its setting—even in places which had formerly been
feared, where a man would fear to walk the road, but in my
days a woman could stroll with hand on spindles, by the grace of
Baal and the gods—yea, there were in all my days plenty and
goodness and good living and ease of heart for the Danunites
and all the Plain of Adana. And I built this city and made the
name Azitawaddiyy because Baal and Reshef-of-the-Stags sent
me to build and I built it by the grace of Baal and Reshef-of-the-
Stags, in plenty and in goodness and in good living and in ease
of heart so that it would be a stronghold for the Plain of Adana
and the House of Mopsh. For in my days there were unto the
land of the Plain of Adana, plenty and goodness; and in my
days it was never night for the Danunites. And I built this city
and made the name Azitawaddiyy. I installed Baal K-r-n-t-r-y-sh
in (it) and offered a sacrifice for every molten image; a head of
large cattle (as) an annual sacrifice, and in the plowing season a
head of small cattle, and in the harvest season a head of small
cattle. And Baal K-r-n-t-r-y-sh blessed Azitawadd with life and
peace and great strength above any other king so that Baal
K-r-n-t-r-y-sh and all the deities of the city might give to Azitawadd length of days and multitude of years and good authority
(?) and great strength above any other king. And may this city
be one of plenty (of food) and wine, and may this people which
dwells in it be owners of large and small cattle and owners of
plenty (of food) and wine, and procreate(?) very much and be
very strong and very obedient to Azitawadd and to the House
of Mopsh by the grace of Baal and the gods. And if any king
among kings, and prince among princes, or person of renown,
who obliterates the name of Azitawadd from this gate and puts
(on his own) name, or even covets this city and removes this
gate which Azitawadd made, and reuses (it) for a strange gate
and puts (his) name on it; whether he removes from covetous-
ness, or from hate and evil he removes this gate; then may Baal
of the Heavens and El Creator of Earth, and the Eternal Sun and
all the Generation of the Gods obliterate that prince and that
king and that man of renown but may the name of Azitawadd
endure forever like the name of the Sun and Moon!

The Phoenicians were an important factor in the Mediterranean throughout the second and first millennia B.C. Their

bilinguals written in mixed communities have been of the greatest value in starting, or refining, a number of decipherments. We shall soon see how the Phoenician version of a Cypriote bilingual provided the key to the Cypriote syllabary. In the summer of 1964 inscriptions on gold were found in Phoenician and Etruscan at Pyrgi, on the Italian coast about thirty miles northwest of Rome. The Pyrgi find is a valuable asset in furthering the decipherment of Etruscan, though the unknown affinities of that language have so far prevented the specialists from ascertaining as much as we would like to know about its grammar and vocabulary. Etruscan is written in a form of the familiar alphabet, so that there is no difficulty concerning the pronunciation. The symbiosis of Phoenicians and Etruscans in Italy early in the fifth century B.C. is in itself interesting. It now appears that the Phoenicians were at an early date on Italian soil, where they could exert direct influence not only on the Etruscans (who, in turn, contributed so much to Roman culture) but for that matter on the Romans themselves.[10]

[10] The partial recovery of the Etruscan language is described by Johannes Friedrich, *Extinct Languages* (New York: Philosophical Library, 1957), pp. 137–43; Doblhofer, *Voices in Stone*, pp. 295–301; Cleator, *Lost Languages*, pp. 167–69.

6

UGARITIC:
DECIPHERMENT
AND IMPACT

All the decipherments we have considered so far have dealt with inscriptions that had been available for some time before they could be read. Some of the breakthroughs were achieved quickly, but the process of attaining a fairly complete decipherment was spread over decades. Ugaritic does not follow this pattern. The texts, in a totally new script, were first found in 1929; the decipherment was effected in 1930.

Ugaritic literature is important in the history of Western

civilization. It has revolutionized Old Testament studies and also bridged the gap between Homer and the Bible.[1] In content, Ugaritic is the foremost literary discovery made so far in the twentieth century.[2] Its impact will eventually be felt at all levels of teaching the origins of our culture, although, as is often the case, the elementary and secondary textbooks used in our schools lag as much as half a century behind the discovery and decipherment.

Ugarit had been completely blotted out of human memory. Its name first reappeared in the Amarna tablets. The rediscovery of its site (which the Arabs now call Ras esh-Shamra, "Fennel Head") was accidental. In 1928 a Syrian peasant, plowing in a field between the mound of Ugarit and the nearby Mediterranean shore, struck a stone slab. It was part of a tomb that archeologists describe as "Mycenaean." Since the area is Semitic and Ugarit is located in northern Phoenicia, the Mycenaean structure foreshadowed discoveries linking the Phoenicians and the Aegean around 1400–1200 B.C. in the latter half of the Late Bronze Age.

In 1929 excavations at Ugarit were begun by the French, who were then governing Syria. The diggers, under the direction of Claude Schaeffer and Georges Chenet, soon found cuneiform tablets, some in Akkadian and others in a new script. The tablets were turned over to an eminent Assyriologist, Charles Virolleaud (born 1879), for publication. He issued the first forty-eight tablets in the new Ugaritic script in the journal *Syria* dated 1929: the same year in which they were found.

---

[1] C. H. Gordon, *The Common Background of Greek and Hebrew Civilizations* (New York: Norton, 1965).

[2] The literary tablets are translated in C. H. Gordon, *Ugarit and Minoan Crete* (New York: Norton, 1966).

The progress of Ugaritic studies is due largely to Virolleaud's character and ability. He prepares the source material promptly for publication. In four decades of pioneering and making basic contributions to Ugaritic studies, he has never been responsible for delays in placing new material in the hands of international orientalists. He has been generous toward other workers in the subject. To cite only one instance, he gave his transliteration of an unpublished literary text to the present writer to be included in the latter's *Ugaritic Handbook*. This kind of generosity is not common. Virolleaud, in addition to his learning, is endowed with a keen eye and a fine hand for draftsmanship, so that his copies are models of accuracy and clarity.

In his 1929 article,[3] Virolleaud laid the foundations for the decipherment not only through making the source material available for everyone to have a crack at but also through some sound observations. He perceived that the script runs from left to right, that the small number of signs (not over thirty) can only represent an alphabet, that a little vertical wedge serves to separate the words, and that the shortness of the words (often represented by only one or two letters) means that none or few of the vowels are indicated in the script.

A group of six signs appeared on some bronze adzes:

(which we now can read: *rb khnm* "the High Priest"). On tablet 18, which has the same format as Akkadian epistles, Virolleaud noted that this group of signs was preceded by a one-letter word ( ):

---

[3] Charles Virolleaud, "Les inscriptions cunéiformes de Ras Shamra," *Syria*, X (1929), 304–10 and Pls. LXI–LXXX.

(which we can now read *l . rb . khnm*). From the epistolary style of Mesopotamia, Virolleaud concluded that 𐎛𐎛𐎛 is a uniconsonantal word meaning "to" (for the epistles regularly begin "To So-and-so"). Virolleaud was right, and although he did not identify the Ugaritic language or assign any phonetic values to the signs, he succeeded in isolating a word and gave it its correct meaning.

A German Semitist, Hans Bauer (1878–1937), soon applied himself to the decipherment of Ugaritic and got positive results quickly.[4] He had been a cryptanalyst in World War I and had also learned some of the basic problems concerning the decipherment of forgotten scripts by working on the Sinaitic inscriptions. Bauer's success was the result of a fundamental assumption: he sensed that the language was Semitic because the words, separated by dividers, are short, a characteristic of the Semitic languages as contrasted with the Indo-European and many other families. Moreover, Syria had long been populated by Northwest Semites such as the Phoenicians, Hebrews, Arameans, and other closely related Northwest Semites. This being the case, the uniconsonantal word for "to" had to be *l*, because *la* means "to" in all the Northwest Semitic languages.

As a seasoned expert on Semitic grammar, Bauer knew that in Northwest Semitic some letters are common as prefixes and some as suffixes. It happens that *t* and *n* are letters of fairly high frequency that serve as both prefixes and suffixes. He found two Ugaritic letters, which we shall call X and Z, that

---

[4] Ugarit and the decipherment of its script are discussed by Leo Deuel, *Testaments of Time* (New York: Alfred A. Knopf, 1965), pp. 224–53; Ernst Doblhofer, *Voices in Stone* (New York: Viking Press, 1961), pp. 203–20; and P. E. Cleator, *Lost Languages* (New York: John Day, 1959), pp. 135–44. Especially valuable is Alan D. Corré, "Anatomy of a Decipherment," *Wisconsin Academy of Sciences, Arts and Letters*, LV (1966), 11–20.

satisfied all the requirements of frequency and position for *n* and *t*, but he could not yet tell which was which. He then noted a list of what looked like personal names, each consisting of three words always with the same two-letter word (for which we shall substitute the symbols "YZ") in the middle. Since Semitic names follow the pattern "A son of B," Bauer read YZ as *bn*, "son." This produced the values Y = *b*, Z = *n*, and (by the process of elimination) X = *t*. Since *b* is often prefixed to words, it fit well for the Northwest Semitic prefix *b* "in." Now Bauer could seek the name of the popular Canaanite god *bᶜl*, "Baal," for he knew both *b* and *l*. He spotted *b*W*l* and concluded that W = ᶜ. There was now no trouble in reading *bᶜlt*, "Baalat" (the feminine of "Baal"), for all the letters had been identified.

In a series of words that looked like numerals, Bauer saw that Q*l*Q had to be "3," written *t̲lt̲* in Arabic. Pattern alone would have sufficed for this identification because there is no cther root in the Semitic languages with the same consonant at the beginning and end and with *l* in the middle. Another numeral, RS*b*ᶜ, could only be *arbᶜ*, yielding two more values. Now the group ᶜ*ttrt* could be read as the name of the goddess Astarte, for all the letters were known. The numeral *a*U*t* could only be the feminine *aḫt* "one"; so that the similar numeral *aḫ*V had to be the masculine *aḫd* "one."[5]

The decipherment of Ugaritic was essentially a problem of monoalphabetic substitution. It was complicated, however, by the presence of three aleph signs (ʾ*a*, ʾ*i*, ʾ*u*), differing according to the vocalization. Also, there are two homophonous signs for *s*. Rather brilliantly, Bauer saw that X*l*YZ, standing parallel to *bᶜl*, was ʾ*ilh-*, "god." He was wrong about the final letter (Z) but right about X and Y, thus discovering another

---

[5] The logic in this reasoning presupposes a knowledge of Hebrew.

aleph (which we now transliterate *'i*) as well as the *h*. He was bothered by the fact that more than one aleph had been revealed through his decipherment, but like a true discoverer he did not let himself get bogged down in doubts; instead, he confidently declared that this "fact" must prepare us for further examples of homophony. Actually, the only instance of homophony in the Ugaritic alphabet is the pair of *s* signs. The alephs are differentiated by the vowels they carry. But Bauer's positive and confident approach made his achievement possible. The kind of perfectionism that makes of every unsolved detail an insurmountable barrier precludes any kind of pioneering work.

Some of Bauer's mistakes were corrected by a French orientalist, Édouard Dhorme (1881–1966), who was not only an able Old Testament scholar and cuneiformist but had also been decorated by the French government for his cryptanalytic services in World War I. Dhorme helped to refine the decipherment not only by correcting Bauer but also by adding the phonetic values of still other letters in 1930. Meanwhile, Virolleaud was working on the decipherment, too. As far as priority in print goes, Bauer published first.[6] Bauer should not

---

[6] He received the issue of *Syria* with Virolleaud's texts and comments on April 22, 1930, identified enough of the letters to get the decipherment started by April 27, informed René Dussaud of his success on April 28, and sent his preliminary report to the *Vossische Zeitung* on May 15. On June 4, 1930, the *Vossische Zeitung* printed his article, in which he claimed to have read at least twenty letters correctly (though in fact only seventeen were right). With the help of Dhorme's corrections and improvements, Bauer wrote up the decipherment of Ugaritic in keeping with what he called his "Alphabet of October 5, 1930" in a book, *Entzifferung der Keilschrifttafeln von Ras Schamra* (Halle/Salle: Max Niemeyer Verlag, 1930), whose introduction (see pp. 1–16) is a masterpiece of decipherment description. Bauer gives a more refined account in *Das Alphabet von Ras Schamra* (Halle/Salle: Max Niemeyer Verlag, 1932). Dhorme's "Le déchiffrement des tablettes de Ras Schamra" has been reprinted in *Recueil Édouard Dhorme* (Paris: Imprimerie Nationale, 1951, pp. 531–36, 767).

be criticized for rushing into print in a newspaper instead of biding his time to appear in a dignified, scientific journal. Such criticism would fail to reckon with a basic characteristic of decipherers: they not only want credit for their accomplishment, but they want to come in first. Second or third place gives small satisfaction to a man with the spirit of a champion.

Virolleaud went beyond Bauer and Dhorme in 1930. In that year more tablets were unearthed, including major literary compositions that were turned over to Virolleaud for publication. Virolleaud's role in the decipherment of Ugaritic may therefore be compared in some ways to Rawlinson's in the decipherment of the Achaemenian inscriptions. Both of these scholars went further than their fellow decipherers because of constant work on a larger corpus of material than was at the disposal of anyone else. We pay our tribute to Bauer, who published his decipherment first (June 4, 1930) and to Dhorme, who improved on Bauer's initial work in an article that came off press about October 1, 1930. But Virolleaud is the Father of Ugaritology for much the same reasons that Rawlinson is the unchallenged Father of Assyriology. On October 3, 1930, Virolleaud's results were announced in Paris at a session of the Académie des Inscriptions et Belles-Lettres. On the twenty-fourth of that month, he addressed the Académie on his methods and on the contents of the newly discovered literary texts. That address, with some revision, forms the basis of his article on the decipherment of Ugaritic in the 1931 volume of *Syria*, in which he came close to achieving the right values for nearly all of the signs in the alphabet.[7] To Virolleaud we owe the first edition and pioneer interpretation of nearly every Ugaritic tablet. His publications since 1929

---

[7] Charles Virolleaud, "Le déchiffrement des tablettes alphabétiques de Ras-Shamra," *Syria*, XII (1931), 15-23.

are coextensive with the history of the subject, from mysterious beginnings to the establishment of Ugaritic as a major Semitic language taught today in scores of universities and seminaries the world over.

The present writer's involvement in Ugaritic began in 1935, after the decipherment was a *fait accompli*. It is only natural that during the 1930s the exciting nature of the Ugaritic tablets should have captured the imagination of many scholars with varying degrees of linguistic preparation. The result was a huge output of literature, in which the student was often unable to separate the wheat from the chaff. Moreover, the burgeoning crop of new scholars interested in the field needed a textbook with a detailed formulation of rules. My *Ugaritic Grammar*, published in 1940, attempted to meet this need. The discovery of new texts and the contributions of many scholars, however, kept raising the general level of the field, so that enlarged revisions of the work appeared; the most recent, *Ugaritic Textbook*, contains not only a grammar but a dictionary, corpus of texts in transliteration, cuneiform reading selections, and other features designed, as the case may be, for the beginner or for the advanced scholar.[8]

Bilinguals turned up too late to contribute anything to the decipherment. One such text is quite interesting. It lists the Ugaritic alphabet and provides the pronunciation of each letter in terms of Akkadian signs. Had this tablet been found in 1929, it would have served as the key to the decipherment. But it was discovered in 1955, a quarter of a century too late to be of any use.

The importance of Ugaritic transcends its decipherment interest and its technical value in Semitic linguistics. Its litera-

---

[8] Published by the Pontifical Biblical Institute, Rome. The book appeared in 1965; in 1967 it was reprinted with a Supplement.

ture occupies a major link in the chain of Western civilization. This is hinted in a type of school text, several copies of which have been unearthed; they are quite little tablets containing the ABC of thirty letters already arranged in the fixed traditional order inherited by the Hebrews, Greeks, and Romans. The Ugaritic sequence of letters has, in spite of the accidents of transmission, come down to us in the order of the following letters: *a b – d – – – h i/j k l m n o p q r s t u/v – – – –*. A study of Ugaritic literature in its Mediterranean setting shows that we have inherited more than just the alphabet from the sphere to which Ugarit belonged.

It was recognized from the start of the decipherment that Ugaritic was closely related to Hebrew and Phoenician. Soon whole expressions emerged, closely paralleling Old Testament expressions. To take only one of many:

ṭl • šmm •	*m-ṭl h-šmym*
šmm • arṣ	*w-m-šmny h-arṣ*
Dew of heavens	From the dew of the heavens
Fat of Earth	And from the fat of the earth

Note that the vocabulary is quite similar; the consonantal skeleton is the same in Hebrew and Ugaritic for "dew" (*ṭl*), "heavens" (*šmm*), "fat" (*šmn*), and "earth" (*arṣ*). Moreover, the poetic parallelism is identical. Instead of rhyme and meter, we find the poetic unit characterized by balanced members: "dew of heavens" is balanced by "fat of earth," for both are manifestations of fertility in the same tradition.

Hundreds of Ugaritic parallels to the Hebrew Bible have revolutionized the study of the Old Testament. The Old Testament scholars took this in their stride. Their field had

weathered the storm of *Babel und Bibel,* and they were used to newly discovered Semitic texts bearing on Hebrew Scripture. It was soon evident that the Hebrews had not invented their language or literary forms; they had inherited them from the older Canaanite population. It was the content rather than the form of the Old Testament that embodied the original Hebrew contribution. Scripture forbids the Chosen People to commit the abominations of the old native population. Some of the abominations—like copulating with animals—are now attested not only in the Bible, which might be considered biased against the Canaanites, but also in the Ugaritic religious texts, where it has a sacred and honored place in the Baal cult.[9] A few Ugaritic texts have been found in Palestine: at Beth-Shemesh, Taanach, and Mount Tabor. There can be little doubt that the kind of literary texts found at Ugarit also circulated in Palestine before the Hebrew conquest.[10]

The academic peace was not disturbed until I pointed out that Ugaritic literature had unmistakable links simultaneously with Homer and the Bible. The Ugaritic Epic of Kret deals with a hero who established his royal line through children whose birth was promised by the gods. The same feature appears in the only other epic found at Ugarit so far, the Epic of Aqhat, in which a virtuous ruler is blessed with a son through divine favor. This is of a piece with the Genesis stories of the Patriarchs, who founded a royal line through the

---

[9] Leviticus 18:23-30; Ugaritic text 67:V:17-22, translated in Gordon, *Ugarit and Minoan Crete,* p. 79.

[10] The Ugaritic Epic of Aqhat is referred to in Ezekiel (14:14; 28:3); see Gordon, *Ugarit and Minoan Crete,* p. 25. That the story was at home in Israel since the second millennium is suggested by the fact that Levi's son Qhat (English "Kohath") is named after Aqhat, while the Hebrew midwife Puᶜah (Exodus 1:15) is named after Pughat, Aqhat's sister (Ugaritic *pûghat* can only correspond to Hebrew *pûᶜah,* by phonetic law).

intervention of God. This is especially clear in the birth of Isaac to Sarah and Abraham.

The Epic of Kret deals also with the recapture by King Kret of his destined bride, Hurrai, from the distant fortress of another king. This is the Helen of Troy motif. What emerged is that in Mycenaean times (in which the epics of Ugarit, the biblical Patriarchs, and the Trojan War are rooted) all the epics deal with royalty and highlight the recapture of the destined bride, for also in Genesis we read that twice Abraham had to get back his wife Sarah from the harems of other kings.[11]

This breach in the "Chinese Wall" that had been erected between early Israel and early Greece inevitably touched off a controversy. Those on the side of the Olympian gods resented Homeric connections with the Northwest Semites. Defenders of Scriptural purity objected to any connection between the Chosen People and the pagans who fought at Troy. But after the criticism had run its course, the plain evidence of Ugarit prevailed and objective scholars accepted the fact that however different classical Greece was from classical Israel, both were rooted culturally in the same Heroic Age during the latter half of the second millennium B.C. The subject is no longer a topic of active controversy. The two categories of interested parties may be described as those who openly recognize the facts and those who have swept them under the carpet. The latter know the facts, more or less, but they would rather not be reminded of their existence.

This peace was not destined to endure, as we shall see in the next chapter.

[11] All these factors are discussed with documentation in Gordon, *Common Background of Greek and Hebrew Civilizations*.

7

THE AEGEAN
SYLLABARY

The earliest inscriptions written
on European soil are from Crete and are generally called
"Minoan." The script started out as pictographic and is sometimes called "Cretan Hieroglyphs." But the most pictorial
inscription that has been found so far is the quite distinctive
Phaistos Disc, written spirally and composed by impressing
dies in the clay when it was still soft. More cursive forms of
the script were developed for common use.

The Minoan system of writing was used for at least two quite different languages: Minoan and Mycenaean. The Minoan texts are called "Linear A" and the Mycenaean tablets "Linear B," following the terminology established by Arthur Evans, who first found both categories of texts at Knossos. However, the system of writing spread outside of Crete to other areas of the East Mediterranean. Mycenaean tablets have been found in peninsular Greece, notably at Pylos and Mycenae. An offshoot of the system has been discovered by Porphyrios Dikaios at Enkomi, Cyprus, from the Late Bronze Age. The system of writing is a syllabary where each sign represents a consonant followed by a vowel. Outside of the economic and administrative texts in Linear A and B, which we shall discuss later, the system is purely phonetic and avoids ideograms and determinatives. The only nonphonetic sign is the word divider, a great help in any decipherment. The system was so strongly entrenched in East Mediterranean culture that it survived in Crete, and especially in Cyprus, until the Hellenistic Age, when it was used in addition to the alphabet.

Around the middle of the nineteenth century, the Duc de Luynes[1] chanced upon some Cypriote syllabic texts and called them to the attention of scholars in Europe in 1852. But it was not until the discovery of a bilingual Phoenician-Cypriote inscription in 1869 that there was a basis for an inspired pioneer to decipher the Cypriote syllabary. The Phoenician text (published by R. H. Lang in 1872) is not intact, but nearly all of it can be restored from other inscriptions of the same monarch, King Milkiyaton of Idalion and Kition. The restored Phoenician text, in transliteration, runs thus:

---

[1] Honoré Theodore Paul Joseph d'Albert (1802–1867).

[*bymm ? lyrḥ ?*] *bšnt 'rbᶜ* 4 *lmlk mlkytn* [*mlk*]
[*kty w'dyl sml*] *'z 'š ytn wyṭn' • 'dnn • bᶜlr*[*m*]
[*bn ᶜbdmlk l'l*]*y lršp mkl • k šmᶜ qly brk*

[On the day ? of the month ?] in the year four 4 of the reign of
  Milkiyaton, [King]
[of Kition and Idalion.] This is [the statue] that our Lord
  Baalro[m]
[the son of Abdimilk] gave and set up [for] his [god] Reshef-
  Mukl, because he heard his voice (and) blessed.

The Cypriote version can now be rendered as follows:[2]

[*i to-i • te-ta-ra-to-i • we-te-i*] *pa-si-le-wo-se •*
  mi-li-ki-ya-to-no-se • ke-ti-o-ne • ka-e-ta-li-o ne •
  pa-si-le-u-
[*o-to-se • ta-ne e-pa-ko-*]*me-na-ne • to pe-pa-me-ro-ne*
  • ne-wo-so-ta-ta-se • to-na-ti-ri-ya-ta-ne • to-te
  ka-te-se-ta-se • o wa-na-xe
[*pa-a-la-ro-mo-se •*] *o a-pi-ti-mi-li-ko-ne • to a-po-lo-ni •*
  to a-mu-ko-lo-i • a-po-i wo-i • ta-se • e-u-ko-la-se
[*e*]*-pe-tu-ke • i tu-ka-i • a-za-ta-i*

[In the fourth year] when King Milkiyaton was rul[ing] Kition
and Idalion on the last [of the] five [inter]calary days, Prince
[Baalrom] the (son) of Abdimilk erected this statue for Apollo
of Amyklai, from whom he had obtained for himself (his)
desires. In good luck!

The direction of the writing in both halves of this bilingual
is from right to left, as is evident from the fact that in the
last line of each, the unused extra space is on the left.

It was George Smith, the Assyriologist, who deciphered
Cypriote writing in 1872 on the basis of this bilingual. First,

---

[2] The transliteration makes it easier for the reader to follow, but the
decipherer, of course, did not know the pronunciation of any of the signs
when he began his study of the text.

he correctly assumed from the large number of signs (about fifty-five) that the script is a syllabary; no alphabet has that many letters.

On seeking the Cypriote rendition of the cluster of three names that appear in Phoenician as *Mlkytn* (Milkiyaton), *Kty* (Kition), and *'dyl* (Idalion), Smith noted that the syllable which we now know to be *li* occurs in the first and third names, now read *mi-li-ki-ya-to-no-se* and *e-ta-li-o-ne*. The identification of the names supplied phonetic values. Matching up the name of Idalion with *X-Y-li-*, we obtain $X = i$ (which we now prefer to transliterate as *e*) and $Y = da$ (actually this sign stands for either *ta* or *da*, and it is now conventional to write *ta*, though *da* is no less correct). The first syllable of the king's name has to be *mi-*, because the *m* is fixed by the Phoenician and the *i* is what indicated the use of the *li* sign to represent vowelless *l*. The royal name also yields *ya*, *to*, and *no*. Smith further observed that *mlk*, which can stand for either the verb "to rule" or the noun "king," occurs twice. This corresponded to the repetition inherent in *pa-si-le-wo-se* and *pa-si-le-u-*[ ]. Smith wrongly assumed that *mlk* is "king" in the genitive on the first occasion but nominative in the second and that the same holds for the Greek. There are a number of errors in this assumption, but it happens that the first of the two occurrences in the Greek is indeed the genitive of "king." Then Smith asked himself, "In what known language is the penultimate syllable different in the nominative and genitive of the word for king?" He decided on Greek, in which the nominative for "king" is *basileus* but the genitive is *basileōs*. In spite of flaws in his analysis, Smith came up with the right identification of the language—Greek; and he correctly identified *ba* (we now prefer *pa*, but *ba* is no less correct because the sign covers *pa* and *ba*), *si*, and *le*.

The few foregoing conclusions and identifications cracked the system so that further progress could be made. Thus, the Phoenician name *ᶜbdmlk* could be matched with the name that we now transliterate *a-pi-ti-mi-li-ko-ne* through the identification of *mi-li* (known from Milkiyaton's name).

Smith established eighteen values with a high degree of probability and proceeded to read Greek names in various Cypriote inscriptions with a fair degree of accuracy. His limited knowledge of Greek prevented him from refining his decipherment. His work was carried on by men with training in classical Greek; first by the Egyptologist Samuel Birch (1813–1885), who had assisted Smith, and then by the German numismatist Johannes Brandis (1830–1873). The finishing touches were made by a succession of Hellenists, and now we have specialists in Cypriote Greek inscriptions such as T. B. Mitford and Olivier Masson. The standard edition of the texts is Masson's *Les inscriptions Chypriotes syllabiques.*[3]

Smith's achievement illustrates a number of phenomena that recur in the annals of the decipherments. Through seeking he discovered truth even though his premises were not entirely correct. He also established the language (as Greek) on the basis of a single word ("king"). A pioneer has to start somewhere, and if he makes a sweeping generalization on the basis of a single word, this is part of the method of the decipherer. Meticulous philologians who cannot get themselves to make a broad inference without a vast array of supporting evidence will never decipher a forgotten script nor reconstruct a forgotten language. A decipherer must guess, but he must have the sense to know when his guesses are wrong, for they will often be wrong, in which case he must

[3] Paris: Boccard, 1961. See p. 246 for the bilingual used by Smith to solve the syllabary.

discard them. It is the lucky guess that pays off. When the lucky guess leads to the breakthrough, the decipherer experiences an illumination comparable to the illumination that mystics know. But the breakthrough must be objectively demonstrable if it is to be accepted as a reality instead of a mirage.

The inscriptions of Cyprus down into the Hellenistic Age are in two languages—Phoenician and Greek. The Greek texts are written sometimes in Greek letters and sometimes in the Cypriote syllabary. The Phoenician alphabet is, of course, used for Phoenician inscriptions. There are also non-Greek inscriptions written in the syllabary, and it is no wonder that a few scholars have suspected that the Eteocypriote inscriptions (as the non-Greek syllabic texts from Cyprus are called) contemporary with the Greek Cypriote syllabic inscriptions are Phoenician. The population may well have used more than two languages, but we know that the main two were Greek and Phoenician. A scholar named A. Mentz tried his hand at interpreting the Eteocypriote version of a bilingual as Semitic, but his readings are wrong. This does not mean that his premise is wrong. Just as we have noted that correct facts sometimes emerge from wrong premises, a correct hunch may be backed up with completely mistaken support, so that the hunch is discredited. Obviously, scholarship cannot treat unproved (though possibly correct) guesses on the same plane as proven fact. The reason Mentz could not get correct readings in the Eteocypriote was not that he lacked perspective, intuition, or intelligence but simply that he did not know enough Semitics or cryptanalysis. The problem must therefore be tackled afresh.

An Amathus bilingual in Eteocypriote and Attic Greek of the fourth century B.C. reads thus:

(Eteocypriote) *a-na* • *ma-to-ri* • *u-mi-e-s[a]-i mu-ku-la-i la-sa-na*
•*a-ri-si-to-no-se a-ra-to-wa-na-ka-so-ko-o-se*
ke-ra-ke-re-tu-lo-se • *ta-ka-na-[?-?]-so-ti* • *a-lo* •
  ka-i-li-po-ti
(Greek) *hē polis hē amathousiōn Aristōna Aristōnaktos eupatridēn*

This bilingual proves that the signs in Eteocypriote texts have the same values as in the Cypriote Greek texts, for *a-ri-si-to-no-se* represents the personal name Ariston mentioned in the Greek. The same holds for the name of Ariston's father, Aristonax, although the Eteocypriote uses the dialectal variant Artowanax (*a-ra-to-wa-na-ka-so-*). Following a Semitic usage, the personal names are accompanied by demonstrative pronouns. These pronouns may be suffixed (*-ose* or *-kose*, "this"), and prefixed pronouns may be used simultaneously: *sa-na a-ri-si-to-no-se a-ra-to -wa-na-ka-so-ko-o-se*, "this Ariston (son of) this Artowanax" (literally, "this Ariston-this, of Artowanax-this").

The Greek version is quite clear: "The city of the Amathusans (honored) the noble Ariston (son) of Aristonax." The verb is omitted as often in such dedicatory inscriptions. But we have an idea of how the people of Amathus honored Ariston. The text is written on a stone with footmarks for holding a statue. The erection of Ariston's statue was accordingly the honor accorded him.

The clearest correspondence between the two versions is at the opening of the text: the first two words in the Greek are "the" and "city"; the same holds for the Eteocypriote: *a-na* (or *hâna*), "the, this" in various West Semitic languages, and *ma-to-ri* (pronounced *madōr* + *ē*) "habitation(s), city." Both versions therefore start with "the city." Since the city did something "for" Ariston, the Semitic preposition *la*, "for,"

is appropriate in *la-sa-na* • *a-ri-si-to-no-se*, "for this Ariston."
The details are discussed in my *Evidence for the Minoan
Language*.[4] The translation of the entire Eteocypriote text is:
"The Amathus-Mukul community, for this Ariston (son) of
this Artowanax—yea this City-of-X, erected(?) this over him
as a memorial monument."

The fact that both the Phoenicians and the Greeks used the
old syllabary into Hellenistic times, long after the introduction and spread of the alphabet, reflects the deep roots of the
syllabary in Cypriote culture. It has therefore occurred to
scholars that there may be a connection between the Cypro-
Minoan tablets found by Porphyrios Dikaios at Enkomi of
the Late Bronze Age (shortly before 1200 B.C.) and Eteocypriote. Some of the signs look alike in both systems, but
other signs do not. Since over half a millennium separates the
Enkomi tablets from the Eteocypriote texts, considerable
changes in form would in any case be expected. Inasmuch as
the trend in Cyprus between the Late Bronze Age and the
Hellenistic period was the growth of the Greek population
and the simultaneous diminution of the Phoenicians, it seems
likely that the Enkomi texts are Phoenician rather than Greek.

The Aegean had been the home of a syllabary since the
Middle Bronze Age. We need not delve here into its origins.
In a world acquainted with various systems of writing, including Sumero-Akkadian Cuneiform and Hieroglyphic
Egyptian, new scripts were bound to appear by the process
of stimulus diffusion. The genetic relationship between the
Cretan syllabary of the Middle Bronze Age and the Cypriote
syllabary of the seventh to third centuries B.C. should have
been obvious from the start. In retrospect, we know that
seven of the signs are the same in form and sound, in both

[4] Ventnor, N.J.: Ventnor Publishers, 1966, pp. 5-7.

sets of texts. And yet the dissimilarity of other signs (mostly owing to chronological and local differences) was enough to prevent the decipherment of the older Cretan syllabary on the basis of the later Cypriote sign forms.

The man who unearthed Minoan civilization was Arthur Evans (1851–1941). Like Heinrich Schliemann, whose faith in the Homeric text had led him to the buried cities of the Mycenaeans, Evans attached weight to the ancient traditions about the greatness of Knossos and of Minoan civilization on Crete. Evans could not accept the common opinion that the splendid culture of the Heroic Age around the Aegean was illiterate. The first step toward his discovery of the Minoan and Mycenaean tablets was his tracking down a group of seal stones that peasants were finding on Crete. They bear signs that are often called Cretan hieroglyphs, dating from the early part of the second millennium B.C. Evans was interested in all of Minoan Crete, but he concentrated his efforts on the excavation of the chief center, Knossos, where he found tablets which could be divided into two main categories that he called Linear A and Linear B. The Linear B tablets are far more numerous, but on Crete they are still limited to Knossos. The Linear A texts, though fewer in number, are found on stone and metal as well as clay at many sites throughout eastern and central Crete.

Evans noted on a Linear B tablet a word of two signs that looked like *po-lo* in the Cypriote syllabary. Since the word was followed by the MANELESS HORSE determinative, Evans compared *po-lo* with Greek *pōlos*, "foal" (cognate with English "foal"). Now we know that this reading is right. Had Evans stuck to it, he would have initiated the decipherment of Linear B, but he rejected it as a coincidence because it did not agree with his theory that Linear B was Minoan

and non-Greek. Any scholar who cannot shake off a false theory is not destined to become a decipherer. However, Evans knew from the rather pictorial signs on the B tablets the objects they dealt with: grain, animals, personnel, clothing, ceramic and metal vessels, chariots, weapons, etc. Such signs serving as ideograms or determinatives can be distinguished from the phonetic signs of the syllabary. The numerals, which follow a decimal system, were also clear to Evans.

Many writers made stabs at reading the tablets; one scholar, A. E. Cowley, suggested that two words (which we now read *ko-wo* and *ko-wa*) might be the Greek words *kouros*, "boy," and *kourē*, "girl," though he confused the genders. Cowley certainly did not anticipate the phonetic discrepancy between the Mycenaean and classical Greek forms of these words, nor did he have any inkling that the second syllable would embody *w* instead of *r*. But it is remarkable that Cowley implied the correct Greek identification of the Linear B tablets, and he did identify a pair of words with the correct Greek pair. But his insight led nowhere because he lacked the measure of dedication to the problem necessary to offset the false non-Greek hypothesis of Evans, who had many followers.

Interest in the decipherment of Linear A and B was widespread because the scripts recorded the earliest historically important documents composed on European soil and were bound to shed light on the emergence of the Greeks in the Bronze Age.[5] It was sensed that the tablets would somehow

[5] The earliest-known European texts are three little unintelligible clay tablets from Tartaria, in Rumanian Transylvania, from the beginning of the third millennium B.C. They are proof of early literacy in the Balkans and suggest connections with Sumer. But beyond this it is hard to evaluate them historically and, as of now, they cannot be compared in importance with the Minoan inscriptions.

be associated with the Heroic Age, when Achaeans and Trojans fought the war that inspired the *Iliad*. Evans has an immortal name among the pioneers in archeological discovery. That he revealed Minoan civilization, even as Schliemann had unearthed Mycenaean civilization, is an outstanding accomplishment that can never be taken away from him. But he also hoped to become the decipherer of Minoan, a task for which he was unsuited. His natural intelligence led him to differentiate sharply between Linear A and B, but his theory that the non-Greek Minoans were the only heroes in the act forced him to identify the languages of the two distinct categories of tablets. The Linear B tablets, as distinct from the Linear A, turned out to be quite Greek. In 1939, when Carl Blegen found many Linear B tablets at Pylos, it became clear that the B tablets at Knossos reflected the conquest of that city by mainlanders. (Later the excavation of more B tablets at Mycenae and elsewhere confirmed this.) But Evans would not face the implications of any evidence that ran counter to his pet theory.

To make sure that no one else anticipated him in the decipherment, Evans withheld the publication of most of the Knossos tablets. Accordingly, his death in 1941 was a necessary prelude to progress. Meanwhile, the war years provided cryptanalytic training for a number of the scholars destined to contribute to the decipherment of Linear A and B. It was a foregone conclusion that the task should start with the abundant B tablets instead of the relatively few A tablets. The addition of the newly discovered mainland texts to the thousands of Knossos texts, now released for publication, gave a new impetus to the challenge of decipherment.

Alice Kober of Brooklyn College performed sound and methodical work on the analysis of the B tablets between

1943 and her premature death in 1950. She did not assign phonetic values or try to pronounce any of the words, let alone identify the language. But methodologically her work was outstanding, and at the time of her death the lines along which she was working were superior to anyone else's. She noted sets of words following the pattern XYZA, XYZB, and XYC and reasoned that the language was inflected with suffixes something like Latin:

a-mi-cu-s
a-mi-cu-m
a-mi-ci

In a syllabary of the Cypriote type, this would mean that the word had three consonants in the stem and that C started with the same consonant as Z but ended in a different vowel.

She noted that there were several such "triplets" of the above type. We shall represent a second set thus: QRSA, QRSB, and QRD. The "A" and "B" here are the same signs as the "A" and "B" in XYZA and XYZB above. For reasons given above, D in QRD reflects the same third consonant that we find in the stem QRS. Kober deduced that C (in XYC) and D (in QRD), though starting with different consonants, ended in the same vowel, on the correct assumption that they illustrated the same inflection:

XYZA : : QRSA (compare *a-mi-cu-s*)
XYZB : : QRSB (compare *a-mi-cu-m*)
XYC : : QRD (compare *a-mi-ci*)

She, of course, did not imply that the endings were those of Latin *amicus* nor that the language was Latin but only that we are confronted with a language of an inflected type, in which the conjugations and declensions required the variation

of the final vowel, the addition of a consonant to the stem, or both.

The method of aligning parallel sets of inflected forms made it possible to chart the signs so that those beginning with the same consonant were on the same horizontal row, while those ending in the same vowel would appear in the same vertical column. Such a chart is sometimes called a "grid," and the method of establishing it is called the "grid system." If we were starting to make a grid on the basis of the above two examples, signs Z and C would appear on the same horizontal row, while signs S and D would appear on another horizontal row, but C and D would be in the same vertical column.

Kober assembled a number of such triplets, including the following in parallel contexts, in the same or similar tablets. The first form modifies the names of women (categorized by the WOMAN determinative); the second form modifies the names of men (categorized by the MAN determinative):

	I	II	III	IV	V	VI	VII	VIII
Form 1:	JKLA	MNLA	OPQA	RSQA	TUVQA	PBWA	XYA	HIA
Form 2:	JKLB	MNLB	OPQB	RSQB	TUVQB	PBWB	XYB	HIB
Form 3:	JKC	MNC	OPD	RSD	TUVD	PBS	XZ	HG

A gifted young English architect named Michael Ventris (1922–1956), who had studied classical and several modern European languages at an early age, heard Sir Arthur Evans discuss an exhibit of Minoan antiquities in 1936. The boy then and there conceived the goal of deciphering the Knossos tablets. In 1940 he published an article proposing Etruscan affinities, nor did he completely shake off this notion until 1952, when he scored his breakthrough and deciphered Linear

B. It was only after sixteen years of thought and frustrating labor that Ventris seriously considered the possibility that the language might be Greek after all.

Ventris reasoned that since Forms 1 and 2 of the above eight words were adjectives, they might well tell the places from which the people came, in which case Form 3 would be the place-name itself without any adjectival suffix.

Now, derived feminine names ending in -$i(y)a$ occur in Greek as well as other languages around the Mediterranean. Therefore, A might be read ya, and the preceding signs (L, Q, W, Y, and I) would end in -i. T happens to be of very high frequency, especially at the beginning of words; it should therefore be a vowel, probably a, which in many languages, including Greek, is the commonest vowel that begins words. It is also clear from the short spelling in Form 3 that the consonant of the case ending (-s) was not written.

Ventris asked himself, "What well-known towns in ancient Crete can be matched with JKC, MNC, OPD, RSD, TUVD? If T = a and TUVD has three syllables after the a-, the town of Amniso(s) comes to mind, so that TUVD is presumably to be transliterated A-mi-ni-so, and TUVQA = A-mi-ni-si-ya. The masculine of the latter, TUVQB, can then only be A-mi-ni-si-yo. ᛏ ⱱ ⵟ ☩ , a-mi-ni-so (Amnisos) was the initial reading that opened Ventris's decipherment of Linear B.

The fact that A-mi-ni-so ends in -o suggests that other place names may end similarly. Therefore, while L, Q, W, Y, and I end in -i, the following have the same respective consonants but end in -o: C, D, S, Z, and G. Now S appears not only as the final syllable in the name PBS but as the second syllable in RSD; the latter is therefore a town name of three syllables

ending in -*oso*. *Ko-no-so* (= Knossos) is the obvious reading because the tablets where this name is found all come from Knossos (and none from the mainland tablets of Pylos and Mycenae). This gives us R = *ko* and S = *no*. The next question is, "What other Cretan town, preferably not too far from Knossos, has three consonants and ends in -*so* (for No. III, OPD, ends in D = *so*)." Ventris's choice of Tuliso[s] (Tylissos) proved to be correct and so yielded O = *tu*, P = *li/ri*.

The character of the Cypriote syllabary was always in the background of the decipherment of Linear B. Actually, seven signs have the same form and sound in the two systems; one of them is the *pa* sign (a vertical line crossed by two horizontals), which we have represented as M in MNC (No. II above). The Cretan town beginning with *Pa*- is Phaistos; this would yield *to* as the value for C (and hence *ti* as the value for L). N was eventually established as the vowel sign *i*; we have *Pa-i-to* for "Phaistos" (for *s* never appears at the close of the syllable). The first name JKC has to be another Cretan town with a name of three consonants ending in -*to*; Lukto(s) (Lyktos), surmised by Ventris, was right, yielding J = *lu/ru* and K = *ki* (where the silent vowel fits in perfectly for forms 1 and 2; *Lu-ki-ti-ya* and *Lu-ki-ti-yo*).

Ventris shrewdly surmised that certain designations common to Pylos and Knossos might refer to guilds, whereas parallel designations limited to either Pylos or Knossos were toponyms (unaugmented or adjectivalized). The names of guilds and towns were to be expected on the analogy of administrative texts from Ugarit.

The phonetic values established by Ventris enabled him to detect Greek words, including some that had been interpreted correctly (although not pronounced nor identified linguistically) by other scholars. For example, Kober had shown that

what we now read as *to-so* accompanies totals of masculine entries (of men or male animals), whereas what we now read as *to-sa* accompanies totals of feminine entries. Ventris could now read them as Greek *tosoi* (masculine plural) and *tosai* (feminine plural), "so many." Moreover, Kober had straightened out the genders of the words we now read as *ko-wo*, "boy," and *ko-wa*, "girl" (first identified by Cowley, albeit with genders confused). In accordance with the orthographic rules formulated by Ventris with the help of his philological associate John Chadwick, *ko-wo* and *ko-wa* stood for dialectal Greek *korwo-s*, "boy," and *korwa*, "girl."[6]

After the decipherment of Linear B as Greek had been accomplished, and the phonetic values ascertained by Ventris were known in the circle of professional Mycenologists, Carl Blegen noted a Linear B tablet unearthed by his expedition at Pylos. It is an inventory of different sorts of pots, with each category described syllabically as well as depicted graphically by a determinative. The latter shows whether the pot is a vase or a tripod and whether it has three, four, or no handles. Applying Ventris' values to the syllabic signs, Blegen found that the verbal descriptions fit the accompanying pictographs in Greek. An examination of the tablet shows that a tripod pictograph followed by the numeral 1 is labeled *ti-ri-po* = Greek *tripou(s)*, "tripod," whereas the same pictograph followed by the numeral 2 is spelled *ti-ri-po-de* = *tripode*—the exact dual form in classical Greek. Vessels with no handles are described on the Pylos tablet as *a-no-we*, "without handle," those with three handles as *ti-ri-yo-we*, "three-handled," and those with four handles as *qe-to-ro-we*, "four-handled." The

[6] The reader will find all the information he needs about Linear B in M. Ventris and J. Chadwick, *Documents in Mycenaean Greek* (London: Cambridge University Press, 1956).

prefixed *a(n)*-, "without," and *tri*-, "three," are perfect Greek; "four" is dialectal and looks more like Latin *quattuor* than standard Greek *tetra*-, but no one should expect Mycenaean Greek to be exactly like any particular previously known dialect.

Ventris's decipherment of Linear B as Greek was not only well done but in general well received. The confirmation supplied by the "virtual bilingual" from Pylos came at just the right time to convince many who might otherwise have hesitated. To be sure, a few doubting Thomases still refuse to accept the testimony of the Pylos tablet, and one scholar went so far as to accuse Ventris of clandestine knowledge of the Pylos tablet. The implication was that Ventris had based his decipherment on that tablet, and therefore his phonetic values had been contrived to describe the pots. Anyone who knows the integrity of Ventris and Blegen cannot imagine them engaging in anything even remotely smacking of skulduggery. There are always those who believe exactly what they want to believe, facts notwithstanding. It is a mistake to take obscurantists too seriously, no matter how learned they happen to be.

The general acceptance of Ventris's decipherment is due also to the desire of those raised in the classical tradition to enhance the glory of Greece. Not that there was ever any reason to doubt that Achilles, Agamemnon, or Nestor spoke Greek. But archeologists had come up with all kinds of theories, and the prestige of Sir Arthur Evans had lent much weight to the notion that Linear A and B were not Greek. Therefore, though Ventris's decipherment was a surprise, it was a welcome and pleasant surprise to Hellenophiles. And what civilized person is not Hellenophile?

The sudden death of Michael Ventris in an automobile

accident on September 6, 1956, snuffed out the life of a talented and fortunate young man. He died after succeeding in his lifework, having received recognition and due honors at home and abroad. The mopping-up operation is being completed by others.

We now come to Linear A, the script that expresses the language of Europe's first high civilization. The A system is essentially the same as the B. There are a number of signs used in A that were not needed in B, because the A language has some phonemes that do not occur in Mycenaean Greek. But nearly all the common phonetic signs of B are found in A. Some names and words are common to both the A and B texts, showing that the same signs have essentially the same pronunciation in both systems; thus, Phaistos is written *Pa-i-to* in A and B texts. As soon as Ventris's decipherment was known, several scholars published monographs on Linear A, based on the correct premise that we can now pronounce most of the A texts and that therefore the A language could be deciphered, provided that it belongs to some well-known family.

As the first important language written in Europe, the Minoan language of Linear A is of unique interest, especially since it is clear that the Minoans provided the cultural pattern (including the script) for the first historic Greeks, namely, the Mycenaeans, whose ways of fighting and living are depicted in the *Iliad* and the *Odyssey*.

Objective linguistic analysis showed, even before the decipherment of Linear B, that the languages of the two sets of tablets were quite different from each other. For one thing, the vocabularies are different, and the words in A are in general shorter than those in B.

This much could be predicted: since B is Greek and A is a

totally different language, the decipherment of A would meet with opposition for the same reason that Champollion's work did. Ventris deserved a cordial and positive reaction because he was right. But, as noted above, that is not the only reason he got it. Those reared in the classical tradition were favorably disposed because the Mycenaeans turned out to be Greek, whereas doubts had been cast on this by the school of Evans. Champollion's decipherment ran into opposition, in spite of the fact that its veracity was crystal clear, because those raised in the classical tradition did not want credit given to a "barbaric" people in the Greek world, and, in a sense, Egypt (especially Alexandria) is part of the ancient Greek sphere. Resistance to identifying those who brought the first high civilization to Greece as "barbarians" is to be expected regardless of the affinities of those "barbarians" and regardless of the evidence and methods used to decipher Linear A. To be sure, there have been efforts to make out some or all of the A tablets as Greek or to identify them as at least some kind of Indo-European. Greek is an Indo-European language, and even affinities with Hittite would at least keep things in the Indo-European family. (Anything to salvage the Aryanism of the earliest great civilization on Greek soil!) Despite the clear archeological fact that the main ties of Minoan Crete are with Egypt, there is an undercurrent of antagonism to the prospect that the Minoans, who brought high civilization to Europe, may have been of Egyptian or some equally unacceptable "barbaric" origin.

As we have already observed, an enlightened Greek, none other than Herodotus, the Father of History, took a different view of "barbarians" such as the Egyptians. Unlike Edith Hamilton, Herodotus saw in Egypt the origin of much that had taken root in the classical Greek world; and he lived in

the fifth century B.C., when Athenian civilization reached its Periclean heights. No one ever loved the Greeks more than Herodotus did, but there was nothing provincial about his outlook.

Up to this point, we have in a sense followed the decipherments from a distance. It is often hard to establish the sequence of progress or the mental processes that led to or refined the decipherments. When Rawlinson was asked how he had arrived at a certain reading (that had subsequently proved to be correct), he used to reply, "How should I know?" This answer need not always have been a device to silence unwelcome questioners. Rawlinson, and others before and after him, may have hit on truth without consciously knowing the mental processes whereby they attained it. The mind is, after all, the most wonderful of computers; Champollion and Rawlinson had over the years fed into their "computers" much varied knowledge that could combine to produce true conclusions. The uninformed observer might explain the process as intuition or lucky guesswork; but when Champollion was able to identify a group of hieroglyphs on the Rosetta Stone with Greek *genethlia*, "birthday celebrations," it was because he knew Coptic and had the kind of mind that combines related data cogently. He sensed that Coptic *misi/mose*, "to be born," must be cognate with Hieroglyphic Egyptian *ms* because the Greek translation *genethlia* left no doubt. He thus established the continuity of ancient Egyptian and Coptic and showed the way on which Egyptology was to proceed. And yet who can now say exactly how Champollion or Rawlinson or Ventris arrived at each step forward?

In the preceding pages, we have read a schematized and simplified account of the first creative steps in the achievements. After a pioneer has gotten his decipherment launched

on its forward march, he may be more interested in advancing it further than in telling how he did it. And if, in order to stake his claims to priority, he tells the story, he may be tempted to color the account in order to strengthen his claims. In any case, it is hard enough honestly to describe what has gone on in one's own mind, let alone reconstruct the thinking processes of someone who died a decade or a century ago. There may accordingly be some merit in my describing the story of the decipherment of Linear A.

In telling the story of the decipherments, it is easier to describe the technicalities of the breakthrough than to fathom what led up to it in the decipherer's past. For this reason, I am inclined to open the account of the decipherment of Linear A with the tale of what I consider to be the main elements in my upbringing and education.

My story starts at home. My father, Benjamin L. Gordon (1870–1965), had received his early education in the Talmudic academies of Lithuania. The atmosphere in which he was raised was one where learning was prized for its own sake. There were, of course, ignorant members of the community, but even they looked up to the scholars as the cream of mankind. The students were not motivated by courses and credits nor by examination grades. They went from academy to academy (without transfer credits!) so as to be where they could learn most at the feet of the masters. When they felt they could profit more under another teacher, they moved on to another academy. Their initial reputations as qualified scholars depended on the reputation of the scholar who certified them. Certification was given when a master considered a young scholar ready to function on his own as a master. The curriculum was limited to Hebrew and rabbinic Aramaic texts. Whatever the program lacked in ecumenical breadth, it

made up in depth and in dedication to the life of learning. My father came to America at almost the age of twenty at the close of the 1880s, and after learning English and whatever else was then required for entering a professional school in the United States, he started his medical education and graduated as a physician from Jefferson Medical College in Philadelphia in 1896.

In his later years my father wrote his autobiography, so that I do not need to tell his life story or eulogize him here.[7] But I should like to note that he was one of those remarkable Victorian individuals who avoided religious obscurantism on the one hand and scientific dehumanization on the other. He cherished traditional learning in its proper place, as well as modern science in its proper place. As a result, I grew up in a home where ancient texts and modern enlightenment were harmoniously intertwined, without the needless extremism of either the William Jennings Bryan or the Clarence Darrow variety.

My foreign-language study began with biblical Hebrew when I was five years old. The values inherent in such a training are many. The content of the text makes an indelible impression on so young a mind, but it has other effects too. For one thing the child learns that there are languages completely different from his own; there are scripts that not only have different letters but may even run in the opposite direction. These facts may not be expressed to the child, but somehow or other they sink in through illustration.

In high school I majored in mathematics but also studied Latin and German, while continuing Hebrew and Aramaic extracurricularly. At the University of Pennsylvania, while

[7] Benjamin L. Gordon, *Between Two Worlds* (New York: Bookman Associates, 1952).

continuing those languages, I added the study of Greek, Swedish, and Arabic.

Swedish played an important role in my linguistic training. My teacher, Axel Johan Uppvall, had a contagious love for his native language. After six weeks of Swedish, I was reading Swedish classics at sight. I had made a discovery: If anybody takes the trouble to look up and memorize every word and to understand every detail of the grammar in the first twenty pages of any book, he can read the rest of the book with scarcely any need of a dictionary. This is so because each author has his own style and mode of expression, which for the most part unfold in any twenty-page sampling of his writing. Having read one book (it happened to be Selma Lagerlöf's *Jerusalem*), I could read any book by the same author; I easily got into other authors (such as Strindberg and Tegner) after mastering the details on the first few pages of one of their books. That I could do this with Swedish inspired me with confidence that I could duplicate the experience with other languages as well. One summer I decided to learn French, Italian, Spanish, Portuguese, Dutch, and Dano-Norwegian by myself, through studying each one of them one hour per day during the three-month vacation. After reading through a grammar of each language rapidly, I would begin to translate a worthwhile book whose contents interested me. Having mastered in detail the first twenty pages, I would read the rest more quickly, looking up only those words whose meaning I could not guess from context. I took sight-reading examinations in the autumn at the University of Pennsylvania and was awarded sight-reading certificates in all of them.

In graduate school I majored in Semitics in a department that required training in all the major Semitic languages as

well as a reading knowledge of Latin, Greek, French, and German. The students were also obliged to study linguistic science outside the department and were encouraged to study Sanskrit because of its value in understanding linguistic science. Emphasis was placed simultaneously on biblical philology and on archeology, along with the study of newly discovered inscriptions. Although there were no courses in history, in their written examinations to qualify for the doctorate, the students were held responsible for voluminous readings in history. The scope of such a program is hard to find nowadays in an age of growing specialization.

I feel a debt of gratitude to some of my teachers, for a variety of influences. One of my Greek teachers, H. Lamar Crosby, conveyed his love of the text of Homer so deeply that the *Iliad* has ever since haunted me. When he read the Greek, or translated it into his dignified English, his resonant voice had a dramatic and melodious quality that made the text unforgettable. Homer became so much a part of me that in later years, when the time was ripe, it came to the fore to combine with my biblical interests and resulted in "Homer and Bible."[8]

I studied Latin, linguistic science, and Old Persian under Roland G. Kent, a meticulous scholar representing nineteenth-century linguistic science with its wholesome stress on phonetic law. Although he helped found the Linguistic Institute of America, Kent was not atune to the voguish innovations of latter-day linguistic schools of thought. He had time only for a few solid novelties, such as the discovery and application of the phoneme. I am convinced that what our students still need is old-fashioned discipline of the Kent variety; only after

[8] Reprinted from *Hebrew Union College Annual*, XXVI (1955); reissued, Ventnor, N.J.: Ventnor Publishers, 1967.

they have mastered phonetic law should they go on to newer and more intriguing developments.

I wrote my thesis under James Montgomery, my ideal of scholar and gentleman. With him I studied Hebrew, biblical philology, Arabic, Ethiopic, and a variety of Syro-Aramaic dialects. He got me interested in Aramaic magic bowls, and I was the only student of his who continued his work in that field. I profited from my magic studies because they helped round out my understanding of antiquity. A conventional education tends to stress the literary, esthetic, and artistic products of the great cultures, so that we come out thinking that every other Hebrew was a prophet and every other Greek was a philosopher. The rank-and-file were plain people trying to make a living and were susceptible to all kinds of unscientific and unspiritual influences that we now brand as superstition and bigotry. Montgomery insisted that his students read history extensively. He was an admirer of the incomparable Eduard Meyer, and my most cherished set of books is Montgomery's personal copy of Meyer's *Geschichte des Altertums* that I have read and reread and refer to constantly.

The thesis I wrote for Montgomery was on the rabbinic exegesis in the Vulgate of Saint Jerome.[9] Jerome (d. A.D. 420) studied with Palestinian rabbis to master the Hebrew Bible in order to translate it correctly into Latin. Jerome's insistence on going back to the sources helped crystallize my natural inclinations along these lines. Jerome was not exactly popular, because of his insistence on getting at the truth from the source itself, but he was uncompromising in his ideals and he has left us a great monument that has stood the test of time. The animosities that he provoked by his integrity and accom-

[9] C. H. Gordon, "Rabbinic Exegesis in the Vulgate of Proverbs," *Journal of Biblical Literature*, XLIV (1930), 384–416.

plishment must have affected my attitude toward the critics of those who do things. To achieve anything outstanding, one must have more confidence in his work and in his ability to perform it than in the critics.

My thesis was hardly a pioneering task, but it was solid and in every way good for me. It made me plow through a lot of Latin, Greek, Hebrew, Aramaic, Syriac, Arabic, and other sources in order to arrive at sound conclusions demonstrable through bona fide evidence. I also was confirmed in my predilection for intergroup cooperation; Jerome left Rome to study with Jewish scholars in Bethlehem. I have made a number of pilgrimages to the Grotto where Jerome is said to have written the Vulgate. He is my kind of saint; his status was not gained by miracles, nor was his sainthood conferred by decree. The sheer weight of his intellectual achievement has won him a place among the immortals not only in the Church but in the annals of secular Western culture, too. Montgomery suggested this doctoral topic, and I accepted it without hesitation. I think he realized that what a young scholar needs is to sharpen his skills by working on sources. Later, when he has mastered his tools, he can go on to bigger things.

I must also mention Montgomery's advice to turn out useful publications, useful in the sense that they help other scholars in their work. When I wrote the *Ugaritic Grammar*,[10] I was following this advice.

My most effective teacher was a martinet—Max Margolis. He was a thorough craftsman and a master of his subject. He was a biblical philologian, working on the Septuagint. His knowledge of the Old Testament text was phenomenal. He expected all his students to recognize any oral quotation from

[10] Rome, 1940.

Scripture and identify it by book and chapter. If he fired a three- or four-word Hebrew quotation at a student and the student failed to identify it, he promptly told the student, "Go to hell!" and went around the room telling each student that failed to recognize the source the same thing, sometimes varying it with "There is room for you, too."

I began to study with Margolis when I was only eighteen, and was more inclined to emulate his erudition than to resent his abusive language. After being reviled before the class a number of times for not spotting his Hebrew citations, I asked him after class one day how I might improve my familiarity with the Hebrew text. He told me to read as much of the Hebrew Bible as I could make time for each day, starting with Genesis 1:1 and reading straight through to the end of the Old Testament. I did this and noticed how many more citations I was progressively able to locate in class.

When I finished the final chapter of Chronicles, I reported to Professor Margolis to tell him the good news. He replied with a faint smile, "Now begin over again." I never forgot the moral; mastery comes only through familiarity with the subject matter. He scorned the kind of scholarship that depended on dictionaries, concordances, and other reference books. There is a place for such books (and his library contained them), but a master has to have the basic knowledge of his field in his head. He used to say, "When you buy a loaf of bread in the grocery store, you do not tell the clerk that you have money in the bank; you have got to lay a coin on the counter. In the same way, no scholar should think that he does not have to know his basic material by heart because he can look it up in concordances and indices. Money in the bank does not take the place of ready cash in the pocket."

Margolis's classes made an indelible impression. A Bible

seminar required the entire apparatus on the large central table. Of course, every student brought his own Hebrew Bible. But on the table were the huge rabbinic Bible, some giant polyglot with the ancient versions, the leading ancient and medieval commentaries, and finally the best modern commentaries. The entire apparatus was scrutinized for each verse read. Naturally it would take a year to cover a couple of chapters, but the student who survived a few years of such a training got something precious that most students lack.

Margolis would ask each student to take on a special assignment, such as a particular version or commentary and be responsible for its evidence. He told me on my first day in class to handle the Syriac version. "But I don't know Syriac," I protested. He looked at me sternly and growled, "Where do you think you are? In a kindergarten? Go home and learn Syriac." Syriac script was then strange to me, but I got a grammar, quickly learned the characters, and found that it is not very different as a language from Aramaic, which I knew. The lesson Margolis rudely taught me stuck. If I need a language, I've got to learn it. And if I have to use a language right away, there is no time to wait for courses to be offered.

The subject that I learned better than any other in all of my schooling was Hebrew linguistics under Margolis. He was not interested in the normal forms of the Hebrew language. For them he told me to read a detailed grammar book, which I should master and use for reference. He taught the underlying principles: mostly accentuation, syllabification, phonetics, and morphology along the most basic lines. Then he would call someone to the board and ask him to write a Hebrew word which happened to be a rare or exotic form. The student would almost invariably botch it and would be called an ignoramus. Then Margolis would draw out of the student the

principles that had been taught and have the student apply them to the form, thus correcting it. Then he would ask the student, "Does this look right?" The student would be afraid to say "Yes" or "No," whereupon Margolis would tell him to look up such and such a passage, and there the form would be in the classical text. This would teach the student to understand and apply the basic principles that were often the mechanical reflexes of syllabification or accent. For Margolis, *Sprachgefühl* meant nothing; texts and texts alone were the criterion. He derived particular pleasure from showing students that they could not trust their *Sprachgefühl* in any language, including their own.

In Hebrew (and even more so in old Phoenician inscriptions) all that is written may be simply the consonantal skeleton. Thus, the reader has to decide, so to speak, whether "dg" is "dog" or "dig" from context; *tht mn wll dg th dtch* is to be read "that man will dig the ditch," whereas *th dg bt th ct* is to be read "the dog bit the cat." Any seasoned Semitist can recognize a familiar Hebrew passage when he sees the consonants. Margolis, of course, could spot any consonantal citation from Scripture by chapter and often by verse. But he had so mastered the structure of Hebrew that he could also spot any biblical verse if confronted with its vocalic skeleton without any indication of the consonants. It is as if one could recognize in *-o- -a-e --e -i--* "God save the King."

In later years, the training he gave me paid off. My ability to formulate in detail the grammar of Ugaritic was largely due to his training.

Another factor that was built into my curriculum as a whole, though it was not the result of any one subject or teacher, was the variety of scripts as well as languages I studied simultaneously. Egyptian, Cuneiform, Ethiopic, as well as

more familiar scripts taught me to read with or without vowels, to know what a syllabary was as distinct from an alphabet, and above all to distinguish language from script. The Syro-Aramaic dialects I studied were all the same language but written in Hebrew letters, Mandaic letters, or any of three quite different Syriac fonts. I was exposed to Judeo-Arabic, the Arabic language in Hebrew letters; and to Coptic, the Egyptian language in Greek letters. Accordingly, I not only wrote grammars of languages in their familiar scripts, but I undertook the reinterpretation of an Aramaic incantation in Babylonian Cuneiform complete with grammar and glossary.[11]

I do not know exactly when the idea of tackling Minoan first occurred to me, but it probably took place during my archeological readings or seminars when I was a graduate student (1927–30). In any case, it was sometime prior to June, 1931, that I conceived the desire to decipher Minoan. I can only surmise the general motivation behind the specific desire. All my teachers stressed the importance of originality. If an article did not have something new, it was not worth publishing. For this reason I have never really had any taste for criticism, bibliography, or summarizing the present status of some topic. I have on occasion yielded to pressures for doing those types of article, and there is nothing reprehensible in doing them, but I have never enjoyed the role of reviewer, bibliographer, or author of encyclopedia articles. In the well-established fields, such as Assyriology, I could make original contributions such as the grammar of the Nuzu dialect,[12] but working out the rules of some dialect of a well-

---

[11] "The Aramaic Incantation in Cuneiform," *Archiv für Orientforschung,* XII (1938), 105–17; "The Cuneiform Aramaic Incantation," *Orientalia,* IX (1940), 29–38.

[12] "The Dialect of the Nuzu Tablets," *Orientalia,* VII (1938), 32–63, 215–32.

known language is not the same as working out a language or a script from scratch. There are degrees of originality, and since I had been taught the fruits of the labors of Champollion, Grotefend, Rawlinson, Hrozný, and others, I felt the urge someday to tackle a major unsolved problem. I was attracted to Minoan because I felt that it was the outstanding major problem. I know I had conceived the desire before June, 1931, because of an incident aboard the old French liner *Patria* that month. I had accepted an archeological field appointment with the American Schools of Oriental Research in Jerusalem and Baghdad, which was to keep me in the Near East for four years (1931–35). In those days before flying had become common, we were fortunate in seeing more by land and sea in our travels. One June night as we were sailing along the coast of Crete, I was sitting with a group of companions on deck, and I was impelled to express my thoughts somewhat as follows, "The Minoan inscriptions from this island are the main challenge to the decipherers of tomorrow. Someone with the necessary knowledge will succeed, through hard and honest work, in deciphering Minoan." In retrospect, I realize that is no way to talk to traveling companions on a moonlit night in the Mediterranean, but I was shamed and silenced by a middle-aged businessman named Mr. Davis, who looked at me with disgust and said, "You sound like a high-school valedictorian." I mention the incident only to bring out the fact that my active concern with the problem twenty-five years later had a quarter-century of brooding (much of it subconscious) behind it.

The archeological years came at the right stage of life. I was young, single, and impressionable. In the Near East I learned to speak a number of the languages—Arabic, Hebrew, French, and German—of which I had hitherto only a reading

knowledge. I became familiar with the realities of "dirt" archeology, and I spent time reading inscriptions on the original clay or stone. The climate and geography of the area with which I was dealing became real to me. My assignments were in Iraq (from Ur in the south to Tepe Gawra in the north), Palestine, Transjordan, and Egypt. The years 1931 to 1935 were relatively good ones in the Near East; the new nationalisms had not yet taken over, and it was possible to travel and cross borders with more freedom than now.

Since 1935 I have spent my life (except for World War II) on a variety of campuses, teaching and writing particularly on the ancient languages and literatures. The four-year hiatus during the war did me much good. Two years of World War II were devoted to breaking enemy codes and ciphers. In addition to doing the work, I also took the home-study courses offered by the Army. The courses laid down the principles and methods; in the work I constantly applied them. The next two years were spent in Iran, where I had the opportunity of seeing western Iran, including Behistun, Persepolis, Pasargade, and Naqsh-e-Rustam.

On returning to academic life, I found I could no longer remain at peace with some of the established dogmas of scholarship. One of the dogmas was the supposed polarity of the ancient Greeks and Hebrews. These two peoples were generally considered to have entirely different backgrounds, as though they had developed in opposite ends of the world, whereas they were both East Mediterranean folk whose history unfolded during the same centuries. The complete separation of Jews and Greeks in the minds of the scholars was not the product of specialized ignorance. All the older Semitists had been educated in classics, and the older classicists were

all at least familiar with the contents of the Old Testament. The dichotomy was dogmatic, and academic respectability required that one adhere to it, at least tacitly. Whether (or to what extent) the "One World" concept that was so much in the air during my formative years had affected my thinking, I cannot say; but I know that my thought does not tend toward compartmentalization. Much of my published work is comparative.

In 1940 my *Ugaritic Grammar* appeared and in 1947 an enlarged and revised edition appeared under the title of *Ugaritic Handbook;* it was followed in 1949 by a volume of translations called *Ugaritic Literature.* My position in scholarship was fixed—or at least seemed so. The image that I had projected among scholars at large (I do not refer to those who happened to know of my full publication record) was that I was a specialist who knew everything about Ugaritic and consequently nothing about anything else. The image was not only untrue, but it irritated me. Even if it were true, a person either grows or dies. I had to look forward. Ugaritic was not to me a blind alley but a key that unlocked several gates.

I had seen in Ugaritic epic a bridge between ancient Israel and Homeric epic. This bridge was not contrived, nor was it of minor significance. It meant a new chapter in the history of Western civilization. My work resulted in the monograph entitled "Homer and Bible," concluding that "Greek and Hebrew civilizations were parallel structures built upon the same East Mediterranean foundation." The reactions were sharp; some of the reviews were lavish in their praise, while others were scornful. But this much was clear: I was no longer a sedate scholar whom specialists accepted as another quiet specialist. I had become a disturber of the academic

peace and at the same time a scholar whose writings and lectures were of interest to a wider public.

My studies of the Greeks and the Hebrews inevitably focused on Crete, the island that is midway between Europe, Asia, and Africa. While my "Homer and Bible" was in its formative stage, Ventris's decipherment was accomplished and confirmed. Scholars who were actively engaged in Linear A and B studies realized that Ventris's solution of B opened the prospect of solving A, but they were unable to identify it linguistically. My active participation in the decipherment began in December, 1956, when I received a copy of *Documents in Mycenaean Greek* by Ventris and Chadwick.[13] One incidental topic struck me as particularly significant: the authors point out that the quasi-bilingual vase-and-tripod inventory from Pylos followed a tradition that the Mycenaean Greeks had inherited from their Minoan predecessors. A Linear A tablet from Hagia Triada (near Phaistos) is also an inventory of pots with syllabic descriptions accompanying pot pictograms. The authors noted that the "vessels are annotated with sign-groups corresponding to Linear B *su-pu* and *ka-ro-pa₃*, cups with *pa₂-pa₃*, *su-pa₃-ra* and *pa-ta-qe*: the difference of language is obvious."[14] This statement rightly implies that the A and B script is essentially the same (at least to the extent that the phonetic signs common to both were read the same way) but that the languages of A and B are quite different, because these vessel names are entirely different from the known Mycenaean vessel names. What struck me was that three of the five Minoan vessel names looked Semitic; *su-pu*, *ka-ro-pà*, and *su-pà-la* (as they can also be transliterated; note that *r* and *l* are not differentiated in the script) resemble

---

[13] London: Cambridge University Press, 1956.
[14] *Ibid.*, p. 328.

the following Semitic vessel names which appear in Ugaritic thus: *sp*, *krp-n*, and *spl*. This tied in with the statement that *ku-ro* in Linear A designated totals;[15] Semitic *kull-*, "all," occurred to me immediately. One should not jump to sweeping conclusions on the basis of four words, but these four Semitic words were evidence suggesting the possible nature of the Minoan language, and I wanted to call this fact to the attention of scholars promptly. I wrote a short article on these four words and concluded that they made it worth probing the possibility that Minoan might be Semitic. I sent it to O. G. S. Crawford for publication in his journal *Antiquity*.

Why I turned to Crawford requires a word of explanation. He had written to me a few years before, concerning Ugaritic. Our correspondence continued, and a friendship grew up bringing with it the realization that we shared interests, attitudes, and standards. Both of us abhorred pedantry. I found in him an archeologist concerned with wide issues as well as with techniques and methods. He found in me a philologian interested in wide issues as well as in techniques and methods. We soon discovered in each other a concern with the origins and development of Western civilization in the East Mediterranean. I wrote and he published an article on "The Role of the Philistines."[16] He had asked me to write on the mature, as against the petty, use of philology. The article I wrote appeared in *Antiquity* under the title "Language as a Means to an End."[17] Crawford was a bit disappointed in my restraint; he felt that a merciless broadside attack on the pedants was in order, whereas I simply stated the case, gave a striking and

[15] *Ibid.*, p. 36.
[16] *Antiquity*, XXX (1956), 22–36.
[17] *Antiquity*, XXIX (1955), 147–49.

new illustration, and let the facts speak for themselves.

Crawford was one of the few creative editors I have known. He played a dynamic role in getting articles that packed some punch. In Britain he was considered a little off-beat but he ran a fine journal, and in a field with its full share of zombies, he was obviously alive. So I sent him my first little article on Minoan, and he replied by return mail that he felt I was on the verge of a major discovery. He said the Semitic nature of Minoan was obvious to him and that I should work on the Linear A texts for a few months and send him a comprehensive article which he would publish in the September, 1957, issue of *Antiquity*. For the remaining half of the winter and all that spring, I spent every minute I could salvage on the Linear A tablets.

The largest collection of Linear A texts are the 150 tablets from Hagia Triada. There are a number of other inscriptions, including eighteen inscribed cult objects of stone, but I could not make much of them at that time on the basis of the published photographs and copies. Accordingly, my early studies on Minoan were based mostly on the Hagia Triada tablets.

My article was called "Notes on Minoan Linear A"[18] and aimed at determining the linguistic family of Minoan. In addition to the three pot names and *kull-*, "all," discussed above, I dealt mainly with personal names such as *da-we-da*, "David." The name *ki-re-ta-na* (var. *ki-re-tá*, *ki-ri-tá*) is connected with "Crete"; I compared it with the Ugaritic hero, King Kret (var. Kretan). I correctly took *ku-pà-nu* and its feminine, *ku-pà-na-tu*, as Semitic, but I reckoned with them as common nouns rather than proper names. (In Ugaritic, the root *gpn* is used to form both common and proper nouns.)

[18] *Antiquity*, XXXI (1957), 124–30.

I discussed and listed nineteen identifications. The soundest ones are the four that I had sent to Crawford in my first, and unpublished, article. Of the others, some are names with cogent Semitic analogues. Other readings were partly or entirely erroneous. My conclusion "that the language of Linear A is a Semitic dialect from the shores of the East Mediterranean"[19] was sound, and it stands without need of correction to this day.

Crawford[20] hailed my article as " 'hot news' of a startling new discovery" concerning the Linear A tablets which I had "succeeded in deciphering."

My next step was retrogressive. I felt that it was not enough to call Minoan "Semitic"; if I was right, I ought to be able to tell what branch of Semitic it belonged to. As I look back over the years, I admit that I was in a hurry to come up with overprecise answers. Where the material is limited, one false identification—or even one serious distortion—can upset the general structure. But comparing Linear A *ga-ba* MAN *62* with Linear B *to-so* MAN *17*, "so many men: 17," I took *ga-ba* to be East Semitic *gabba*, "all," and translated the Linear A passage "all the men: 62." The damage done was not that I had misinterpreted a word (for *gb* "all" turned up a decade later in Ugaritic text 601:5) but that I threw the whole problem off balance. The short article in which I stated this was called "Akkadian Tablets in Minoan Dress."[21] At least one new reading in it has stood the test of time, *a-ga-nu*, which is the opening word on a text written inside a little clay bowl; I pointed out that it was the Semitic word *'aggānu*, "bowl." Shifting the identification from West to East Semitic impeded

[19] *Ibid.*, p. 129.
[20] *Antiquity*, XXXI (1957), 123.
[21] *Antiquity*, XXXI (1957), 237-40.

but did not altogether stop progress (for the Semitic languages are closely related). It will be recalled that the grammar and vocabulary of Akkadian (East Semitic) were worked out so thoroughly largely on the basis of Hebrew and Arabic, which are West Semitic.

A South African classicist, Maurice Pope, supported my identification of Minoan in the guise of an attack. He showed that ⅀ ⌇ 𝖤 *ku-ni-su* (which Furumark had correctly defined as "wheat" because of its WHEAT [𝖳] determinative) appeared in Akkadian as *kunnišu*. Pope also gave examples of *u*, "and" (which occurs in Akkadian), in addition to those I had published. These look distinctively Akkadian, but as a matter of fact they are also found in West Semitic, if one knows where to seek them. Another South African classicist, S. Davis, at first supported my Semitic identification in a friendly manner. But both abandoned their support as criticism of my position persisted. Pope then assumed a negative posture of complete neutrality; for him Linear A might be Indo-European, or Semitic, or something else. Davis later made Minoan out to be Hittite, a positive position more in keeping with the mood among quite a few classicists.

A priori, Akkadian was not a bad guess as a written language in the East Mediterranean. We know from the Amarna Letters (and countless other tablets from elsewhere in the Levant) that around the middle of the second millennium B.C., Akkadian was the written language *par excellence* in the whole area (where, by the way, Akkadian was not spoken)—in Palestine, Phoenicia, Syria, Anatolia, Cyprus, etc. But in cryptanalysis, while guesses are necessary, wrong or unprecise guesses must be abandoned if progress is to be made. As long

as I was hampered by the East rather than West Semitic identification of Minoan, few advances were possible. In 1958 I published "Minoan Linear A"[22] and in 1960 "The Language of the Hagia Triada Tablets."[23] In neither of these articles did I make any notable progress. It was not until the end of 1961 that two publications enabled me to extricate myself from a frustrating deadlock that had dragged on for four and a half years.

Toward the close of 1961 I received my copy of W. C. Brice's new edition of the Linear A texts.[24] Brice is not a philologian, and his interest in such matters is largely mechanical. Above all he likes to turn out tidy work, and he did so in this book. In addition to supplying photographs, he provided neat, stylized India ink copies of all the Minoan texts. Moreover, he compiled forward and reverse indices of all the word groups (in the original script only), including names as well as vocabulary words. His normalized copies of the religious dedications were of special value to me. Hitherto I had neglected those documents partly because of their illegibility and partly because I had felt that the Hagia Triada tablets were better to work with, since they are the largest single group of Minoan texts. But the religious texts have a value that the Hagia Triada tablets lack; they contain sentence structure, with evidence for the verbs and the syntax. As long as I dealt only with the Hagia Triada tablets, the critics could and did say that all of the Semitic words might be loanwords.

---

[22] *Journal of Near Eastern Studies*, XVII (1958), 245–55.
[23] *Klio*, XXVIII (1960), 63–68.
[24] W. C. Brice, *Inscriptions in the Minoan Linear Script of Class A* (New York: Oxford University Press, 1961).

The very appearance of Brice's copies was enlivening. Going over the *editio princeps* time after time had had a stultifying effect. While perusing Brice's copies and indices, I was struck by a word in a votive inscription. Brice (who had no linguistic theory) copied it as a sequence of four signs that are read 𐀹𐀄𐀅𐀪 *ki-re-ya-tu*. The first and third signs are so defectively preserved that Meriggi had transcribed the word *?-re-?-tu*. But Brice's keen eye detected the traces of the *ki* and *ya* signs. Now *ki-re-ya-tu* is the perfect Minoan spelling of the *West* Semitic word *qiryatu*, "town, city." East Semitic uses an entirely different word: *âlu*. Hebrew, Ugaritic, Aramaic, and Arabic all use forms of *qiryatu*. Moreover, the feminine singular ending in the nominative (*-atu*) confirmed the Semitic grammar of Minoan. As soon as I recognized *qiryatu*, I realized the error of my East Semitic theory and got back on the right path that I had unfortunately abandoned in 1957.

I wrote up the new developments in an article called "Minoica," which was published promptly in the *Journal of Near Eastern Studies*[25] by the editor, Keith C. Seele. I must single out this editor for his courage because my decipherment was considered controversial.

I pointed out in "Minoica" that since *qiryatu* points to the West Semitic affiliation of Minoan, other elements were becoming clear. The text in which *qiryatu* appears begins with *re* followed by a word which is very common in the votive inscriptions. This should be West Semitic *le* = Arabic *li*, "to, for," a common and idiomatic introduction for votive formulas (in Hebrew the form is *la*, which becomes *le* in open unaccented syllables not directly before the accent). (In East Semitic *ana* is used instead of *le*.) The text ends *ki-te-te-bi*

[25] *Journal of Near Eastern Studies*, XXI (1962), 207–10.

ki-re-ya-tu, "so that the city may thrive," which makes sense and is intelligible against the background of Ugaritic, Phoenician, and Hebrew. Accordingly, I had at last been able to read virtually an entire inscription (insofar as it has been preserved) with a preposition, conjunction (introducing a purpose clause), a verb, and a noun (with proper Semitic suffixes for feminine gender and nominative case). Moreover, the preposition and noun made it clear that the Minoan language was West Semitic akin to Ugaritic, Phoenician, and Hebrew. In the same article I also identified the West Semitic word for "wine" (inscribed on a Minoan wine pithos from Knossos) and the demonstrative pronoun *za,* "this," used syntactically as in Phoenician.

But simultaneously something else had happened. Davis, who had abandoned my camp, had just come out with a monograph: *The Phaistos Disk and the Eteocretan Inscriptions from Psychro and Praisos.*[26] He now interpreted the whole range of Minoan as Hittite. His readings are often quite un-Hittite, and his reasoning is circular and proves nothing, but he did something of great importance. He rightly implied continuity of the Minoan language from the pictographic Phaistos Disc through Minoan down to the Eteocretan texts (from Praisos and Psychro) in familiar Greek letters that range from 600 to 300 B.C. I could make nothing of the Eteocretan texts so long as I approached Minoan as East Semitic. But now, at the beginning of 1962, that I had found my way back to the West Semitic identification of Minoan, I saw the Eteocretan inscriptions in a new light. Whole sentences became clear, such as *me u mar krko kl es u es* [   ], "whosoever he be, lord of his city, every man and man [   ]," meaning "anybody, fellow citizen or otherwise." This concept is repeated in

[26] Johannesburg: Witwatersrand University Press, 1961.

another Praisos text in partly different wording: *nas iro u kl es*, "the people of his city and any (other) man." Moreover, the Psychro inscription perpetuates the dedicatory terminology attested in Minoan over a thousand years earlier.[27]

Seele asked me to review Davis's monograph, which I gladly did, not to criticize Davis but to honor him for his "courage, boldness and enthusiasm—qualities without which real problems can never be solved."[28] I asked Seele to let me republish the Eteocretan texts with my notes as a review article. Seele agreed and it appeared under the title of "Eteocretan"[29] directly following "Minoica."

What had happened so suddenly was of prime importance, for now we possess a continuation of the old Minoan language in a familiar script that poses no difficulty of pronunciation. Thus, the advantage of having more Minoan (although very late Minoan) texts was enhanced by the familiarity of the Eteocretan script, which could only help clarify matters.

The changed picture early in 1962 ushered in the present phase of the decipherment of Minoan, which has been characterized by steady progress. It soon became clear that the two main readings (*u*, "and"; *ku-ni-su*, "emmer wheat") on which the East Semitic identification had been based are attested also in West Semitic. No obstacles were left to block the right road.

An important Eteocretan inscription on stone was found at Psychro, where the Dictaean Cave is located. The text, in Greek uncials of about 300 B.C., begins ΕΠΙΘΙ (*epithi*).

---

[27] The details in the decipherment of Eteocretan and Minoan are available in both technical and popular form, e.g., C. H. Gordon, *Evidence for the Minoan Language* (Ventnor, N.J.: Ventnor Publishers, 1966) and Gordon, *Ugarit and Minoan Crete*, Chapter III, respectively.

[28] *Journal of Near Eastern Studies*, XXI (1962), 211.

[29] *Ibid.*, pp. 211–14.

After the Eteocretan text, the scribe rewrote the opening
word in a late form of the Minoan syllabary: *i-pi-ti*. This
bigraphic[30] inscription shows that the Minoan syllabary was
remembered on Crete, as on Cyprus, into the Hellenistic Age,
at least at the site of one famous ancient Minoan shrine, where
a conservative priesthood maintained old ways through chang-
ing times. Two Bronze Age libation tables inscribed with
Minoan dedications come from the Dictaean Cave. Thus, the
tradition (including script as well as language) lasted there
from the Bronze Age deep in the second millennium, until
after Alexander the Great.

The Psychro stone perpetuated the Minoan terminology for
dedications on stone. The opening formula is   ΕΠΙΘΙ Ζ
ΗΘΑΝΘΗ (*epithi z ēthanthē*) = Phoenician   𐤓 𐤍𐤋𐤐𐤇
𐤍𐤋𐤍ʾ (*ḥ-ptḥ z ytnt*), "this engraved stone I have given." In
ancient Minoan the same wording is used: *pi-te za*, "this engraved stone"; the Eteocretan *ēthanthē*, "I have given," is
the same verb as Minoan *a-ta-n(o)* or *ya-ta-n(o)*, "he gave" =

Phoenician   𐤉𐤕𐤍 (*ytn*). Thus, the tie-in with Phoenician
and the linguistic continuity from Minoan to Eteocretan are
established. All this jibes with the ancient Greek traditions
that the Minoans were Phoenician. Indeed, Minos is represented as the son of the Phoenician princess Europa. Even as
late as the fourth century A.D., a Latin author, Lucius Septimius, records that the old language of Crete was "Phoenician."

After the demonstration that Minoan-Eteocretan was
Northwest Semitic, two Eteocretan-Greek bilinguals from
Dreros, Crete, came to my attention. They had been buried
in classics publications where Semitists in an age of over-
specialization had paid no attention to them. The Eteocretan

[30] I.e., in two scripts but in the same language.

version of the first Dreros bilingual ends ∧ M O (*lmo* =
Hebrew *l'immō*), "for his mother," corresponding to the dialectal Greek MATPI (*matri*), "for [his] mother." Semitic
-*m*- (= Hebrew *'ēm*), "mother," and the distinctive West
Semitic *l*-, "for," and -*ō*, "his," clinched matters. Moreover,
an accusative in the Greek TON TYPON (*ton tyron*) corresponds to a noun in Eteocretan introduced by ET = ♪✕
(*et*): the sign of the accusative regularly in Hebrew and
sometimes in Phoenician. The Greek of the second Dreros
bilingual established the Northwest Semitic verb "to be"
(cognate with Hebrew *hāyā*, "he was") in Eteocretan.

The Northwest Semitic vocabulary of Minoan-Eteocretan
leaves no doubt as to the classification of the language. It
includes "the, this, his, for, and, all, it will be, he gave, I gave,
I set up as a votive offering, mother, man, people, friend,
companion, city, town, engraved stone, wheat, seven, nine,
ten," and at least four names of ceramic vessels. The grammar
is good Semitic. All this is now recorded and documented in
technical as well as popular form.[31] All that I claim to have
established is enough of the vocabulary and grammar to set
the decipherment of Minoan on its right course.[32] More texts

[31] My popular article on "The Decipherment of Minoan," *Natural History*,
November, 1963, pp. 22–31, was solicited by one of those rare creative editors, Mrs. Helene Jordan.

[32] There is no dearth of scholars who recognize this. Armas Salonen, *Die
Hausgeräte der alten Mesopotamier (Gefässe)*, (Helsinki, 1966), incorporates
the Minoan ceramic terminology in his important book (II, 49, 91, 111,
125) and classifies Minoan as a Semitic language in the index (II, 432).
Other competent Semitists who understand the evidence and recognize the
Semitic character of Minoan include M. Astour, *Hellenosemitica* (Leiden:
Brill 1965); D. Neiman, *Journal of Near Eastern Studies*, XXV (1966),
46; J. Sasson, *Journal of the American Oriental Society*, LXXXVI (1966),
128; and E. Yamauchi, *Journal of the American Oriental Society*, LXXXV
(1965), 517; and *Journal of Near Eastern Studies* XXV (1966), 95. Among
the Semitists who have joined their ranks in 1967 are: J. J. Glück, "Some

are being found and eventually literary documents may come to light.[33]

In addition to Northwest Semitic names, the Minoan tablets contain non-Semitic names of various derivations. Some are Egyptian, tying in with the archeological evidence of close relations between Minoan Crete and Egypt. This is in agreement with Greek legends that derive the early Phoenicians from northeast Africa. Belus and Agenor were twin brothers sired by Poseidon out of Libya. Agenor left Egypt to settle in Canaan, where he married Telephassa (also called Argiope), who bore him Cadmus, Phoenix, Cilix, Thasus, Phineus, and a daughter, Europa. Belus remained in Egypt and begot twin sons, Danaus and Aegyptus. Danaus became king of Argus in Greece, and the Greek heroes proudly called themselves *Danaoi* for a long time in his honor. The sum total of the evidence (epigraphical, legendary, and archeological) points

---

Linguistic Problems of the Near East in the 2nd Millennium B.C.," *Taalfasette: Taalkongresverhandlinge*, III (Pretoria: J. L. van Schaik, Beperk, 1967), 53–56 (see p. 54); and H. Haag, "Der gegenwärtige Stand der Erforschung der Beziehungen zwischen Homer und dem Alten Testament," *Jaarbericht*, XIX (Leiden: Ex Oriente Lux, 1967), 508–518. See especially the detailed review of *Evidence for the Minoan Language* by F. Díaz Esteban in *Sefarad* XXVII (1967), 125–27. Moses Hadas, in *The Greek Ideal and Its Survival* (New York: Harper & Row, 1966, p. 17), fits the Semitic character of Minoan into the development of Hellenism, and Edward McNall Burns, in *Western Civilization* (New York: Norton, 1963, p. 131), fits it into the outline of world history.

[33] It is inconceivable that the Minoans, as a literate people in a world that cultivated written belles-lettres (Egyptian, Ugaritic, Akkadian, Hittite, etc.), had no literary texts. There is reason to believe that the Minoans wrote not only on clay and stone but also on soft and perishable materials such as lime bark, specifically for recording literary texts (Arthur Evans, *Scripta Minoa* [Oxford: Clarendon Press, 1909], I, 109). Lime bark would not last indefinitely if exposed to moisture. It is always possible, however, that someday Minoan inscriptions on soft materials will be discovered in dry caves on Crete, such as those in which the Dead Sea Scrolls were discovered in Palestine.

to the Delta of Egypt as the homeland of the Minoans, who gained control of Crete and erected the early palaces there in Middle Minoan times (about 1800 B.C.). Another group of Northwest Semites, the Hebrews, also migrated from the Egyptian Delta, though at a later date (roughly 1200 B.C.). The fact that both the Minoans and the Hebrews are Northwest Semites from the Delta explains much of the common background between early Greek and early Hebrew civilizations. Let us consider an example that embodies such a cluster of elements that accidental similarity is ruled out:

In the eleventh book of the *Odyssey*, Odysseus consults the spirit of the deceased prophet Tiresias to learn what the future holds in store and what he should do. He goes to *Erebos*[34] to inquire (*puthesthai*) of the dead.[35] Similarly King Saul inquires (*sheōl*) of the spirit of the dead prophet Samuel to find out what is in store for him and what he should do.[36] The use of the word *sheōl* (= *puthesthai* in Greek) tells us why the Hebrews called the underworld Sheol: the living could inquire there of the dead even as Odysseus and Saul consulted the spirits of Tiresias and Samuel. Now *Erebos* means "west"[37] in Semitic, though it reflects the Egyptian concept that the west is the abode of the dead. The reason that the Egyptian designation reached Greece in Semitic translation is that the term came via Semites from the Delta.

The pattern (as distinct from the content) of Hebrew and Minoan civilization is the same to a remarkable extent. In both traditions, the Law was revealed by God (or Zeus) on a sacred mountain (in Sinai or Crete) to his human favorite (Moses or

---

[34] *Odyssey* 11:37.
[35] *Ibid.*, 11:50.
[36] I Samuel 28:3–20.
[37] *Odyssey* 12:81.

Minos), who was aided by a divinely inspired craftsman (Bezalel or Daedalus).

The content of Hebrew and Minoan civilizations is by no means the same, largely because Hebraism is a conscious reaction against Canaanite-Phoenician values. For example, the worship of animals, including the bull, is strictly forbidden in the law of Moses; and yet the fact that Israel repeatedly lapsed back into the worship of the golden calf[38] shows that the Hebrews were emerging from a milieu, like that on Minoan Crete, characterized by bull and calf worship.

The decipherment of Minoan is important for understanding the great civilization that gave the Mycenaean Greeks their headstart. It also explains the common denominator uniting Hellas and Israel in the second millennium B.C.[39]

Since the contributions of the Greeks and Hebrews combined to lay the foundation of Western culture, it is worth noting that the combination is not a schizophrenic union of two unrelated and alien systems. To the contrary, the birth of our Western culture is rather the blending of two parallel structures (the Greek and the Hebrew) built on the same East Mediterranean foundation.

[38] Not only in the days of Moses and Aaron but also later at the north Israelite shrines of Bethel and Dan (I Kings 12:28–29).

[39] Concerning the linguistic character of Minoan, note also George Bass, *Cape Gelidonya: A Bronze Age Shipwreck* (Philadelphia: American Philosophical Society, 1967), p. 167: ". . . the conservatism of some authorities in accepting Cyrus Gordon's discovery that Minoan (Linear A) was Phoenician (Northwest Semitic) has been based largely on their inability to see Semites in the Aegean during the Bronze Age. Our present study offers independent archaeological evidence which disproves the conservative views."

8

SUMMATION AND PROSPECT

We have surveyed the decipherments that have pushed back the written history of Western civilization to about 3000 B.C. The texts that have been opened up derive their significance from the light they have shed on the Mediterranean background of our culture. No linguistic group has monopolized the stage. The Sumerians have the best claim to priority in the march of high civilization. Through Akkadian they made a great impact on other cul-

tures: Hurrian, Hittite, Canaanite, Aramean, etc. Via the West Semites, notably the Arameans, Sumerian influence was brought to bear on Arabic, whence Islam carried the heritage from Spain to Indonesia. And yet, until the decipherment of Akkadian, the very name of the Sumerians had been obliterated from human memory.

Akkadian is particularly important. As an international language, like Latin in Catholic Europe of the Middle Ages, Akkadian was used as a *lingua franca* in western Asia, Egypt, and the East Mediterranean, including Greece and Cyprus. The fact that Akkadian belongs to the well-known Semitic family has enabled scholars to work out its grammatical and lexical details with finesse. From about 2500 B.C. to the dawn of the Christian era, Akkadian supplies us with more inscriptions for reconstructing history than any other deciphered source.

The Hurrians until the decipherment of cuneiform were only a name; they are the Horites of the Old Testament. No one realized that they were a major group of people spread over the Near East, including Anatolia, the Aegean, and Egypt, throughout the second millennium B.C. Hurrian studies are progressing slowly because the language is not related to well-known groups. Urartean, which is akin to Hurrian, moves ahead still more slowly because the Urartean texts are more limited in number and scope.

Cuneiform Hittite is well established because the script is the familiar Sumero-Akkadian system of writing, with definable ideograms and pronounceable phonetic signs. Its Indo-European character has not only made it linguistically clear, but it has in turn shed light on the nature and development of the Indo-European languages that embrace English. On the other hand, Hieroglyphic Hittite is still imperfectly read be-

cause of difficulties in the script and limitations as to quantity and variety of texts.

In spite of the limited content and number of the Old Persian texts, their language has been worked out thoroughly, thanks to its close relationship to the other Indo-Iranian dialects of the Indo-European family.

Egyptian is of great importance because it is the language of the most influential land on the Mediterranean shores for most of recorded history from 3000 B.C. to Alexander's conquest. Egyptian literature includes the world's oldest literary prose; the early prose narratives of the Old Testament are indebted to it for style. Since both the Minoans and the Hebrews migrated from the Delta to Crete and Palestine, respectively, Lower Egypt can be called the cradle of both the Greek and Hebrew cultures.

Ugaritic is so closely related to Hebrew and the other Semitic languages that it is fairly well known, and the remaining obscurities are being cleared up steadily. Ugaritic has a more direct bearing than any other language on Old Testament studies, and it has bridged the gap between early Greek and early Hebrew literatures. Moreover, Ugaritic has, more than any other subject, pointed the way to the decipherment of Minoan.

The Aegean syllabary is of unique significance because it expresses the first important written languages of Europe and provides the cultural background of the Greeks on what became Greek soil. Although the syllabary (as well as the contents of the Minoan texts) reveals Egyptian influence, the basic character of the script is not Egyptian. The main thrust of the Minoans may have come from Egypt but not from Upper Egypt; they hailed from the coast of the Delta, which is Mediterranean in more ways than one. The Minoans were a

sea people, and it is possible that there was a peri-Mediterranean script that the Phoenicians (and perhaps other sea people too) used and transmitted not only to the Aegean but wherever they sailed or settled.[1] This whole subject needs to be investigated.

Mycenaean Linear B is being employed for elucidating early Greek language and cultural history. Minoan Linear A is identified as Northwest Semitic, and though its texts are limited in number and scope, the very fact of its identification will have a major effect on our understanding of ancient history. There is hope that literary texts in Minoan will be found. A poetic tablet from Enkomi, Cyprus, of the Late Bronze Age shows that the Aegean script was used for literary texts. Moreover, there is an account of the discovery of literary texts at Knossos during the reign of Nero. Nero, by the way, knew they were Phoenician and called in Semitists to translate them. They are represented as containing the story of Dictys of Crete, a hero of the Trojan War. The account comes from Lucius Septimius, who lived in the fourth century A.D., and his story as well as his Latin rendition of the Greek translation were condemned as spurious. After the condemnation, however, papyri of earlier date were found in Egypt giving an older Greek version of Dictys Cretensis. It will be no surprise if, as has happened so many times, the ancient sources are correct, and the Greek was translated from the Semitic original that had been found at Knossos and transmitted to Nero, who was known for his intellectual pretensions.

[1] The dedicated work of the late A. Morlet, culminating in his *Glozel: Corpus des Inscriptions* (Montpellier: Causse et Castelnau, 1965), deserves sympathetic and careful study. While I am not yet in a position to decide whether the Glozel texts are genuine, it is my feeling that some of the suspicion and disdain of the scholarly world in this case may have been prompted by the will to rule unwelcome evidence out of court.

There are many facets to the Aegean syllabary. Greek and Northwest Semitic texts were written in it on both Crete and Cyprus. The most interesting single text in what seems to be the same system is the attractive Phaistos Disc in pictographs. A beginning has been made in reading it,[2] but there is a lot of work ahead before it can be called deciphered. It is not out of the question that the Aegean syllabary may have been used for languages other than Northwest Semitic and Greek, for there are many texts in Linear A and B as well as in the Cypriote syllabary and Cypro-Minoan that have not yet been read meaningfully.

Etruscan is of special interest because it provides background on Italian soil for Roman history and culture. The golden texts in Etruscan and Phoenician, of the fifth century B.C., from Pyrgi on the coast thirty miles northwest of Rome, should contribute something to the decipherment of Etruscan. However, the obscure affinities of that language will keep us from understanding it in detail until we find long and varied bilinguals. Meanwhile, the most interesting result of the Pyrgi text is the fact of the Phoenician presence in Italy long before the Punic Wars.

The horizons opened up by the decipherment of Cuneiform, Egyptian, and the other scripts we have reviewed bring home to us the deep roots of our culture. Long before Moses led the Children of Israel out of Egypt or Agamemnon sailed with his troops to Troy, great literary civilizations in Mesopotamia and Egypt had laid the foundations of our arts, sciences, humanities, religion, ethics, law, and economy. The Minoan synthesis in the Middle Bronze Age did not take place until after Egyptian and Mesopotamian literacy had gone through a

[2] C. H. Gordon, *Evidence for the Minoan Language* (Ventnor, N.J.: Ventnor Publishers, 1966) pp. 40–41.

millennium of high achievement. The earliest known Greeks and Hebrews came still later, in the Late Bronze Age. The glory of Israel and Greece, therefore, is not that they created their cultures *ex nihilo* but that they eclipsed qualitatively the brilliant civilizations that provided them with their headstart.

All this means that our heritage is the product of cosmopolitan enlightenment, and to understand it requires knowledge and study. It embodies the highest ideals to which we may aspire. Our most serious challenges today are often the fulfilment of biblical or classical ideals. International peace was first formulated by Hebrew prophets who sensed that it can only be realized when weapons are supplanted by productive tools and men abandon warfare as a way of life: "They shall beat their swords into plowshares, and their spears into pruning hooks. Nation shall not lift sword against nation, nor study the art of war any more."[3] This is not a primitive or outmoded idea but a landmark in human thought. It towers above the ideals of Egypt and Mesopotamia that had preceded it in written form by over two millennia. It is still relevant, more urgent today than when it was enunciated in the eighth century B.C.

Nor is there anything passé or primitive about Aristotle's logic. It is just as much of a goal that we must try to reach as when it was first composed in the fourth century B.C.

No heritage in history is superior to the Western tradition. It requires historic depth and intellectual keenness to appreciate it. The decipherments of the forgotten scripts are making our biblical and classical heritage more meaningful than ever before. Herein lies the challenge to deciphering the known unsolved systems awaiting their Grotefends, Youngs, Champollions, and Rawlinsons and other systems yet to be unearthed in the years to come.

[3] Michah 4:3.

INDEX